Tough Mind, Tender Heart

Reflections on a Black Woman's Activist Journey

Sandra Barnhill, JD

Copyright © 2024

All Rights Reserved

Disclaimer

All rights reserved.

No part of this publication may be reproduced, distributed, or transmitted in any form or by any means, including photocopying, recording, or other electronic or mechanical methods, without the prior written permission of the copyright owner, except for the use of brief quotations.

Although the publisher and the author have made every effort to ensure that the information in this book was correct at press time and while this publication is designed to provide accurate information in regard to the subject matter covered, the publisher and the author assume no responsibility for errors, inaccuracies, omissions, or any other inconsistencies herein and hereby disclaim any liability to any party for any loss, damage, or disruption caused by errors or omissions, whether such errors or omissions result from negligence, accident, or any other cause.

Dedication

I am deeply grateful for my village. In every stage of my life, I have found my people—those who nurtured, challenged, walked with me and sometimes dragged me forward with love and struggle.

My family, an example of unwavering resilience, has shaped my values and beliefs and inspired me to push the boundaries of my activism.

The matriarchs and patriarchs, whom I learned about through the elders in my family, were enslaved yet lived and died free and have been a constant source of inspiration. My mom, Carrie Lampkin Barnhill, taught me my earliest lessons about walking tall. 2023 marked the twentieth anniversary of her death, and I still hear her voice, which speaks loudly to me during times of adversity.

My sister, Tanya Barnhill Turnley, has been my biggest cheerleader. When we were little kids, Tanya, older than me, always kept her eye on me. She protected me from bullies, fought for me when needed, and shared everything with me. She lived up to the elder sister's role; even today, if she finds me in an uneasy situation, she would step in to rescue me. I love her for that and for the fact that no matter how wild or unconventional my ideas are, she never fails to encourage me and help me think things through and strategize, showing me the power of unwavering support through good and bad.

Others outside my immediate family are "my people" and members of my village. They have played an equally important role in my life.

The two women, Paula Dressel and Dola Young, who were incorporators of AIM (Aid to Children of Imprisoned Mothers), now known as Foreverfamily; the nonprofit earth angel, Delvia Hart Fisher, who gave me my first office space free of charge; and the healer, Janie Asante, who provided her services at no charge guided by the philosophy of Ubuntu. This philosophy, rooted in the African tradition, emphasizes the interconnectedness of all people and the importance of community.

It was a guiding principle in the counseling she provided to the children and families the agency served. The college professors helped develop our pedagogy and theory of change and grounded them in an Afrocentric and womanist perspective.

The board members, staff, interns, and volunteers who for over three decades served with me riding buses long distances to prisons, waiting outside in lines, going through metal detectors, laughing and crying with parents and children as they visited Children's Centers and general visitation areas, enduring bugs, heat and no sleep in south Georgia for Camp AIM High, a transformative residential summer experience for the children we served, planning Back to School parties and funding field trips to museums, civil rights centers, and other historical sites, helping with homework in the afterschool program, leading the Umoja

Circle, writing grants, planning 5K races, speaking at events, entertaining early and late night calls from me about the work, dreaming with me about what could be and most of all, holding sacred the trust the children and families had in us and in the organization we built not off the backs of those we served but through hard work, a deep belief in and commitment to our cause. Their acts of love, grace, and service enriched my life and built an organization with a strong legacy.

I dedicate this book to them, appreciating their invaluable contributions and recognizing their role in my journey.

Acknowledgments

The purpose of a book acknowledgment is to allow the author to recognize and celebrate the many people and organizations who, at different stages, were involved with the book's creation. You, the reader, are not just a part of this journey but a significant contributor to its success.

I wrote this book for you in the hopes that you would not just read it but share the message that we can all be activists and work in some way- large or small to make the world a better place.

This book is the outgrowth of my learning and development in the independent sector space. Much of my growth came from my direct service work, which I discuss in the book. A lot also came from my intentional time away to focus on myself, recharge, and have opportunities to expand my thinking through engaging with people and new experiences and reading books, articles, and materials provided in my fellowships.

In 1996, I met Ralph Smith, the senior vice president of the Annie E. Casey Foundation, who now heads the Campaign for Grade-Level Reading. I met him at a conference (I cannot remember what the conference was about), and I didn't agree with much of what he said in his presentation. Being me, I went up to him afterward and shared some of my thoughts, which diverged from his.

He told me he thought I would be great for a fellowship program at the Casey Foundation, and he wanted to send me an application so I could apply. I said thanks, but no thanks; I was about doing real work on the frontlines, not being in some navel-gazing program. He laughed and didn't give up. He not only sent me the application, but he kept in touch with me, always gently reminding me that there were two sides to everything and that I could do more for change if I broadened my perspective.

To make a long story short, I did apply for the fellowship and got accepted. Ralph became my assigned mentor in the fellowship program, and our talks, my externship experiences during the program, and the nine other men and women who made up my 1997 Fellowship class changed my life significantly. I will always be grateful to Ralph and the Casey Foundation.

In 2004, I also completed a fellowship with the Ford Foundation called Leadership for a Changing World. While that fellowship is now defunct, it also changed my thinking and life. As did the 2020-2021 Encore Public Voices Fellowship, where I learned to write op-eds and was able to publish two op-eds that reflected where I was in my work at the agency and my consulting business.

In 2011, I started working on the book during a social justice artist-in-residence at Kalamazoo College; many thanks to Dr. Jaime Grant, who I met during my 2004 Leadership for a Changing World fellowship. She was the founding Executive Director of the Arcus Center for Social

Justice and chose me to be their first activist in residence. While there, I started working on the book and co-taught a class with her on social justice fundamentals. I was on leave from my nonprofit, which provided me with a chance to rest, write, and do research. After my residency, The Arcus Center provided a summer intern who helped me create the website for the book, conduct more interviews, and continue to focus on the book.

In 2012-2013, The Children and Family Fellowship Network created by people who, like me, were in the Casey Foundation fellowship program, supported me by providing a mini-grant that allowed me to continue working on the book. Over three years, I interviewed over 40 activists, listening to their stories and featuring many of them on my website, Tough Mind, Tender Heart (toughmindtenderheart.com).

If you visit the website, you will see their names and some of their stories. Some of the activists remain on the battlefield, continuing to work on their social justice issues, and others have gone on to do other things, but each made a difference on an issue for a period of time.

During those years , I also developed an initial draft of the book. I am deeply grateful for the support and feedback I received from Paula Dressel, Kweku Forstall, and Atiba Mbiwan on the earliest draft. Their insights were invaluable and showed me that I had much work to do.

Then life started "life-ing," and I took an 11-year hiatus from the book. Much of that was because my work at Foreverfamily, the non-profit I founded, became very demanding, and funding to buy time off to write dried up. I could not do both, so I chose Foreverfamily—a decision I will never regret.

So much of what I write about in this book is shaped by my 37-year journey at the agency. In the book's dedication, I pay tribute to my AIM (Aid to Children of Imprisoned Mothers, an agency that became Foreverfamily) "village"- those who supported me through almost four decades of work. I will not spend time here talking more about that. Still, I want to acknowledge that my professional career and life have been shaped by work on the ground with real people, and every step of the way, it has been people over programs, places, and things.

In 2020, COVID provided me with more at-home time, and I started working on the book again; my thoughts about what the book should be had changed, and many thanks to Kim Brundridge, who helped me think about the direction I wanted the book to take. With her support and prompting, I began working on another book version. Paula Dressel, who also gave feedback on the initial draft, read it and challenged me to put more of myself- my life and my stories- into the book.

The world reopened in 2022 after the COVID scare. I once again had to move away from the book. I began grinding—working at a breakneck speed that included leading a nonprofit agency and continuing to run a consulting business whose work had picked up during the COVID years.

In the fall of 2022, I read Tricia Hershey's book *Rest is Resistance: A Manifesto* and thought about how much "grind culture" had shaped my professional and personal life. I spent 2023 thinking about the book and praying for balance, guidance, and direction because I wanted to finish the book.

In January 2024, I started working on the book again but took the work up differently. I made a plan that involved retiring from the agency I founded, streamlining my consulting work, and committing to a summer spent focusing on rest and writing. I was intentional about not talking about the book but working on the book and adhering to the plan.

On February 15th, after 37 years, I retired from Foreverfamily. A fantastic woman, Camilla Ngurre Paul, now heads the agency. I continue to work as the CEO of my consulting firm, Sandra Barnhill & Associates (sandrabarnhillassociates.com). During the summer of 2024, in honor of all my years of work and a dire need to rest, I instituted a two-month, no-work-related travel policy and shortened workdays for June and July. I said no to personal and professional opportunities that would not allow me to have the summer to rest and write.

Don't get me wrong.

I still worked for those two months, but it was a four-day workweek, and I took a vacation- no, I didn't board a plane or go to a hotel. I had a staycation. Occasionally, I saw friends, but I made myself a priority. Resting gave me the energy to work on the book, so I spent lots of time on my deck, my happy place, and painting, which clears my mind and calms my spirit, thinking, and writing.

I also hung out, especially on Sunday, at the pool. The activities I described above helped me do an internal reset and gave me the bandwidth to end a 13-year writing journey.

I am grateful for the support and guidance of Breshkai Davis, an outstanding book coach who has challenged me and asked probing questions that have clarified my goal for the book and helped me find my voice in the writing.

I want to give special thanks to two of my thought partners and close friends:

Paula Dressel has walked this journey with me for over four decades. I met her when she was my Sociology professor at Georgia State University. Of course, I had to challenge her over a study she shared in class and its purported findings about Black people.

That day in class, she showed herself genuine by listening and acknowledging the limitations of white researchers who come into the Black community to gather data but never involve the people they are researching to analyze that data. She has supported my various jobs and social justice endeavors, from serving as a mitigation witness when I worked as a lawyer to serving as the inaugural president of the agency I founded in 1987.

In 2023, after semi-retiring, she returned to the agency's board to be the vice president, leading the strategy work around public policy. We have seen each other through marriages and divorces, traveled the world together, and always kept it real about white supremacy and white privilege.

She is the author of the *Race Matters Toolkit* and the co-founder of a 501 (c) (3) called *Just Partners* (justpartners.org), where she has led their racial equity work and challenged white people, herself included, to do their work.

Donovan Duncan is a rich blend of intellect and heart. I met him at the Casey Foundation when he came up for his fellowship interview. We hit it off, and the rest is history. He joined the board of the agency I founded over 12 years ago, served as its vice president, became its president, and currently serves in that position.

He shepherded the agency through my departure as the founder. It has been my honor to be his ally in the trenches. I am grateful for the countless hours we spend discussing the independent sector, social change, our commitment to Black people thriving, and the work that must be done to heal our world. Our candid conversations have shaped my thinking and influenced this book.

About the Author

I am a Southern Black woman who has been consumed with what it means to live in a "just" world since the age of eight. As a kid, I saw the disparities between the 'haves' and the' have-nots' and thought we could improve things and correct every wrong. As an adult, I still see those disparities.

I believe we can make things better. I am unsure about righting every wrong, but I think we have a role to play or, in simpler terms, work to do if we want a just world.

My deep love for people and intimate knowledge as a Black woman of what it means to be marginalized have helped me understand the need to remain committed to justice work. I have spent my entire career in the independent sector working on social justice issues—first as a lawyer, then as an activist and organizer.

Some people see activists and organizers as the same thing, but I don't. You can be an activist—championing issues and causes, working on the frontline, and raising public awareness about injustice without being the one doing the organizing work.

Early in my career, because I worked on an issue that was not on people's minds, the children affected by parental incarceration, I did a lot of organizing. The role of an organizer is to figure out how to bring diverse people together around a common issue or agenda. That work is about dismantling the notion of othering, breaking down barriers, and creating spaces of belonging so that many people can connect to the issue and mobilize. Sometimes, you must organize things before you can activate them.

I have operated in and between those two roles and will always honor each. Folks can do one or both because they go hand in hand, and we need both roles fulfilled to make a change. Each requires a tough mind and a tender heart.

Ultimately, my goal has been to create what bell hooks*, an amazing Black woman truth-teller who came back home to the South during her later years, often talked about in her writing—creating a space, a place where we can live fully and well and where everyone can belong.

*Name lowercase at the author's request.

Preface

I have been an activist for over 40 years, beginning in college. Back then, there were no instruction books or blueprints for being an activist; today, there still aren't. Some say we don't need a blueprint for activists because our work is ever-evolving. While that might be true, we do need those of us who have been organizing for causes and doing movement-building over the long term to talk about our work, the joys, the challenges, and the realities of it in honest and practical ways so that there is a narrative that comes directly from our lived experiences.

Hopefully, by doing that, many of the myths about activism and the false narratives about those of us who do the work are debunked.

In movement work, we talk a lot about *"speaking truth to power,"* which we describe as speaking out and up about injustices, challenging the status quo and those in authority and the practices they propagate, and uplifting a different way. This new direction is more equitable and focuses on the change we want. I have spent my career speaking truth to power in that way. Yet, I recognize that I rarely talk about what it requires to speak truth to power, to stay the course. I hope this book shares some of that.

More than anything, I want more people to engage in activism. I am looking at the full spectrum of activism, from those who want to do it as a full-time career to those with a burning cause they wish to support. Even if they cannot commit to activism as their full-time job, they can give volunteer hours, and their activism can range from writing a letter about an issue to attending a march, rally or signing a petition. To make this world better, we need people who, in many different ways and levels, take action to create social change. That is what activism is all about in its broadest sense.

Those who do this work full-time must talk more about their work and how they have done it. This is not to create a blueprint but to show that there are many ways to make change, and in the process of making change, we make a life, do important work, and grow through the process.

This commitment to transparency and honesty is crucial to extending our invitation to others. This means we must go beyond allowing TV docu-dramas or "Savior Sagas" that gloss over reality to serve as recruitment tools for those who want to join the movement, whether full-time or episodic. There must be a greater understanding of the internal work required if you want to work for justice and do it in a way that does not reflect the actions of the systems you are trying to dismantle.

My organizing work has been on the frontlines, working at the deep end, a place that demands resilience and determination. The deep end is where you break new ground, bringing issues that are invisible or relegated to the background to the forefront and addressing injustices that stem from the *"isms"* in our society that we don't want to address.

That deep-end work has less support, fewer victories, more contradictions, and staying the course over long periods is challenging. But it's in these deep-end experiences that I discovered who I was and where my strength and resilience came from, inspiring me and hopefully others, to keep pushing forward. Deep-end work builds character and can build a whole new cadre of activists. Yet, when people hear about working at the frontlines, they shy away because they believe it requires too much. All they hear about are the martyrs, not the ordinary people who are working in the deep end.

It's not a place where sheroes and heroes in their pristine capes quickly find the answer, save the day, and change the world. In the deep end, kryptonite comes in the form of racism, sexism, imposter syndrome, scarce resources, and burnout. Pondering what you will sacrifice or do for the almighty funding dollar is negotiated daily, and going to scale is the world's litmus test for agency viability. It is where the rubber of our lives meets the road. It is where we need the most work to garner the most change!

In this book, I share my journey as an activist. I talk about what drew me to activism—a deep belief in justice and a desire to find a place where I am accepted— the challenges I have faced as a Black woman working in the independent sector, which is still white and male-dominated at the highest levels. I share personal anecdotes of the discrimination I faced and the strategies I used to overcome them.

I also discuss what it means to be a founder and build a nonprofit organization from scratch, undergird it with Afrocentric, womanist, people-centered, and community-based practices, and sustain it for almost four decades on a minimal budget because the right to self-determination of the children and families I served often conflicted with those entities that wanted to fund us and that funding required that we accept their prescriptive notions about how we needed to do the work.

I also share what I have learned about myself, the work, the practices that have sustained me as an activist, and the great joy and fulfillment I found in working for a cause that was so powerful that I was willing to make sacrifices to do it.

Finally, I end the book with my hopes for the future and the work ahead. It seems important to share that at this pivotal time in our history. No matter what side of the political spectrum you are on, the 2024 presidential election will influence the future of this nation and the world.

Those of us who want peace and justice must continue to work to build a better future for ourselves, our families, our local communities, our nation, and the world community. As I look ahead, I am filled with hope and optimism, knowing we can and will make a difference together.

What I share on these pages will encourage you to be an activist, even for a few hours. Your involvement is not just desired; it's urgently needed.

Contents

Chapter 1: Roots of Activism

Throughout history, Black activists have stood on the frontlines of the struggle against racism, courageously confronting injustice and demanding change. The poet and civil rights activist, Maya Angelou once declared, *"You may encounter many defeats, but you must not be defeated."*

These words resonate with a profound truth—that the journey toward justice is often fraught with obstacles and setbacks, but it is worth undertaking. In this chapter, I talk about my upbringing and the ways it shaped me and started me on a journey that is lifelong.

From the earliest days of my childhood, I have borne witness to the injustices wrought by systemic racism in my own lived experiences and the broader context of society. Raised in a household that prized pride in our Black identity, I was keenly aware of the barriers and biases that shaped our daily lives. My parents, especially my mother, had a great influence on me. She was born in the 1920s in the deep South in a whistle-stop town called Appling, where her family had been proud Black farmers and her great aunt, Aunt Rena Lampkin, was a midwife. They instilled in me an unwavering belief in myself and a relentless pursuit of excellence.

My family's heritage was a source of pride for us, yet the world outside displayed a brutal reality. Brown v. Board of Education had been decided a few years before I was born. In the early years of my life, Ruby Bridges and the Little

Rock Nine all challenged the new law that said separate but equal was unconstitutional. Rosa Parks refused to sit in the back of the bus, and there were sit-ins in Greensboro and other cities. Black Americans, buoyed by the acts of Black men and women who fought in WWII, came home and wanted equal treatment and were willing to march, fight, demand, and, in many cases, die for their rights.

As a child, I felt that the high moments of the civil rights movement had all passed. That, of course, was not true, but all of the stories I heard about the challenges Black people faced and the bravery they exhibited as they claimed their rights made me so proud and also made me wonder why we weren't free and equal yet. That is a question, I have spent my life asking and trying to make sure the answer was one I could live with.

Serious, intense, and driven—these words have consistently defined me, and my approach has always been one of taking charge. Being in charge doesn't necessarily imply always being right, but it does entail being ready to make decisions and forge ahead with determination. Mostly, this approach has served me well, but sometimes it didn't.

I preface this story by highlighting our early initiation into travel. At age ten, my father's military assignment took us to Germany, and the entire family relocated with him. Consequently, venturing abroad and navigating unfamiliar territories became second nature to my sister, Tanya, and me, devoid of any apprehension or fear.

I recall a trip to Italy where a colleague and I were slated to speak at an international conference focusing on children of incarcerated parents, and my sister joined us. Somewhere along the journey, a pivotal moment arose when we were supposed to change trains, yet somehow, the message didn't quite register with me. Tanya may have hinted, "Shouldn't we switch here? Many passengers are disembarking."

I confidently replied, "No, this isn't our stop."

Consequently, we remained on the train. At that time, there wasn't a direct high-speed route from Rome to Milan, which complicated matters. As the train reached its terminus, it became apparent that we should have descended earlier, prompting us to backtrack. I vividly remember the incredulous look Tanya, my colleague, and I exchanged. The silent exchange spoke volumes, conveying a shared thought: the issue had been raised earlier, but my unwavering confidence had dissuaded any further inquiry.

I downplayed the situation, pretending it wasn't a significant mishap, but I knew it was a big deal deep down. Exhaustion weighed heavily on us; hunger gnawed at our stomachs, and our sole desire was finally reaching our destination. After enduring a grueling 9.5-hour flight from Atlanta to Rome, navigating customs, retrieving our luggage, and locating the train, the prospect of backtracking meant additional hours spent on the train. We were drained, hungry, and utterly weary.

I often think to myself that in handling the train situation and the subsequent inconvenience, Tanya had various options available to her; she could have asserted herself as the big sister, the older authority, but instead, she chose to approach it as she had throughout our lives by extending grace to me.

This dynamic also extended to my relationship with my older brother, William Hill, who has since passed away. He, too, extended grace toward me – often defined as unmerited favor. This sense of grace reminds me of how important it is to extend grace to ourselves and others. Something that seems in short supply in our world now.

Throughout my life, I've frequently found myself adopting the same posture I had on that train to Milan. As a Black woman, this posture often reflects a response to the world's expectations that I cannot simply wander through life aimlessly. There's an implicit understanding that I must always have a destination, a purpose, and a clear path to reach it. If I don't adhere to these expectations, I become susceptible to the rapid reinforcement of stereotypes commonly associated with Black women.

As I think about how Black people have to show up, I am reminded of Paul Lawrence Dunbar's poem, *We Wear the Masks;*

We wear the mask that grins and lies,

It hides our cheeks and shades our eyes,—

This debt we pay to human guile;

With torn and bleeding hearts, we smile,

And mouth with myriad subtleties.

Why should the world be over-wise,

In counting all our tears and sighs?

Nay, let them only see us, while

We wear the mask.

We smile, but, O great Christ, our cries

To thee from tortured souls arise.

We sing, but oh, the clay is vile

Beneath our feet, and long the mile;

But let the world dream otherwise,[1]

We wear the mask!

---

[1] https://www.poetryfoundation.org/poems/44203/we-wear-the-mask

I remember reading that in middle school; it was in a collection of poetry that was in our house. Reading was expected, and my parents made sure we read books by Black authors.

Paul Lawrence Dunbar wrote the poem in 1895 when Black people were dealing with the personal and political aftermath of the Civil War, which might have legally ended slavery, but the oppression and repression of Blacks continued.

I have spent a lot of my life wearing the mask – smiling when I felt like crying or masking my true emotions to protect myself. The older I have gotten, the less willing I am to wear the mask because to do so is to be complicit with a system that is designed to dehumanize me and other people of color.

I went through a period in my activism where I would not cry no matter what. I perceived my crying as me letting "them" win. I didn't realize that not crying was letting them win because crying is an expression of our humanity. Things would happen, and I would just stuff all those emotions.

Being vulnerable is an important aspect of being human, but as a Black person, a woman and as an activist, I learned that there was no room for that in my life. It was during that time that I noticed my joy was gone. I started earnestly praying and asking God to give me back my joy and to make me tender again. God did, using a great Black woman therapist with an Afrocentric practice that spoke to my soul.

I see many activists who have given their lives to the fight for justice and, in the process, lose their joy. I hope for them what I continually hope for myself- that we will figure out, as my fore parents who faced unimaginable challenges as enslaved people, how to have joy. The first step on the journey to that joy is recognizing that we can do this work of justice without losing what we wanted to obtain from the beginning- a better life for ourselves and others.

I believe that a better life begins with finding balance that allows us to work hard, rest, and replenish our minds, bodies, and spirits.

I talk a lot about that in this book, using my experiences to remind activists- entrenched and emerging- that we can be well while doing good.

In 2011, I was the first activist-scholar at the Arcus Center for Social Justice at Kalamazoo College. I went to a lecture on campus, and I cannot remember who the speaker was, but the person shared all these statistics. Each one was worse than the one before, and they were all about Black people. I remember I started to cry, and the presenter stopped- shocked, really. There was an uneasy silence, and then they started talking again. Afterward, one of the students came up to me and said they couldn't believe that I was crying. I said hearing all those negative things about Black people deeply affected me, and my heart was breaking, and I could not hold that pain in.

It is not unusual for people to see me cry and sometimes weep. I openly say my tears are powerful, and shedding a tear means I am alive and well. I hope I will quit work if I ever reach a point where I cannot cry again.

In my household, my mother firmly believed in children knowing their place. Yet, it was not the confines of my home that restricted my ability to experience childhood freely. It was the broader societal interactions—be it at school or through extracurricular activities—where I faced the stark reality: society often fails to see Black girls as just that, girls. This reality is highlighted by more recent statistics that underscore the disproportionately harsh treatment Black girls face, particularly in educational settings.

For instance, during the 2017-2018 school year, despite Black students constituting only 15% of the K-12 student population, they accounted for more than 30% of those who faced suspensions, expulsions, or arrests—a stark reflection of disciplinary disparities. Specifically, Black preschoolers, who made up 18.2% of the enrollment, represented 43.3% of all out-of-school suspensions and 38% of all expulsions, highlighting that such disparities begin at an incredibly young age (USAFacts).

The broader implications of these disparities are profound, indicating a systemic issue within our educational system that goes beyond individual instances of misconduct. These statistics suggest a pattern of behavior from educational institutions that not only unfairly targets Black students but also has lasting impacts on their educational journey and perception of their place in society.

Despite some progress in reducing overall suspensions and expulsions over the past decade, the persistence of these disparities underscores the need for a concerted effort to address the root causes of this inequity. This includes reevaluating disciplinary practices and policies to ensure they are applied equitably across all student demographics, providing training and resources for educators to handle disciplinary issues without resorting to exclusionary practices, and fostering a school environment that recognizes and respects the dignity and humanity of every student, regardless of race.

The challenge is not insurmountable, but it requires acknowledgment, commitment, and action from all stakeholders involved in the education system to create an environment where every child can truly be a child, unburdened by the existing biases and barriers.

For this reason, nearly 40 years ago, I founded and managed a youth development agency. Throughout this time, I witnessed Black children, particularly Black girls, often lacking the freedom and flexibility to simply be themselves. Through the work of our nonprofit, Foreverfamily (previously known as AIM - Aid to Children of Imprisoned Mothers), I aspire to have created that much-needed space for little Black girls (and boys, too) to embrace their true selves—to feel comfortable being uncertain, unsure, and okay with that.

The narratives this world has for little Black girls have shaped a lot of who I am and how I show up in the world.

My family's expectations also shaped who I was as a Black girl and how I showed up. In the next section, I share some of the experiences that grounded me and developed me into a doer and a dreamer.

Chores were a regular part of life in our home. Weekdays were dedicated to working for my parents and for us, attending school, while weekends were reserved for household cleaning and completing assigned tasks before venturing out to play. The only exception to this rule was if you had school-related obligations, in which case you were exempt from chores. I made sure to involve myself in every club and extracurricular activity offered by the school, which often meant leaving for school-related events on Saturday mornings and skipping the cleaning duties at home.

Even now, I still loathe cleaning! You won't catch me tidying up the house on a Saturday. What bothered me most was the gender disparity in household chores—the fact that it was always the women who were tasked with cleaning, while the men, including my dad and brother, never seemed to lift a finger to mop, vacuum, wash, or fold clothes. Even during the holiday season, the women were left to polish the silverware.

I wasn't familiar with the term "equity," but I sensed something wasn't fair. While I didn't expect us all to have identical chores, I believed there should have been a more balanced distribution of tasks. Nowadays, "equity" has just become a buzzword in our society. I appreciate the way the

National Association of Colleges and Employers (NACE) defines it:

Equity means recognizing that we do not all start from the same place and must acknowledge and make adjustments to imbalances. The ongoing process requires us to identify and overcome intentional and unintentional barriers arising from bias or systemic structures.[2]

As a young girl, I began to fight against the expectation that women must handle all the housework before pursuing anything else. This struggle persists today, with many women bearing the brunt of domestic responsibilities at home. In the United States, women typically spend around 2 hours and 15 minutes per day on household activities, compared to men, who spend about 1 hour and 25 minutes on average.

I'm pretty sure that marked the beginning of my journey as a "womanist," a term I embrace now. Alice Walker didn't coin it until 1983, but even back then, I was acutely aware of the prevalent sexism within my household and society at large. During my high school years, the term women often used was "feminist." While I identified with it initially, I eventually realized that as a Black woman, it didn't wholly capture my experiences or reality.

Dr. Layli (Phillips) Maparyan introduced me to womanism when she served on the board of the nonprofit I

---

[2] *Equity Definition.* (n.d.-b). Default. https://www.naceweb.org/about-us/equity-definition#:~:text=What%20is%20Equity%3F,and%20make%20adjustments%20to%20i mbalances.

founded. Her book, *The Feminist Reader* (as Layli Phillips), was released in 2006 and is an anthology documenting the first quarter century of womanist thought from an interdisciplinary perspective. She joined the agency's Board of Directors in 2009 when she was an Associate Professor in the Women's Studies Department at Georgia State University (GSU) and remained on the board until 2011, a year or so after she had taken on a new position where she remains as the Executive Director of the Wellesley Centers for Women and Professor of Africana Studies at Wellesley College. She is an expert on the womanist worldview and activist methodology.

During my school-age years, there were numerous groundbreaking moments for women. I vividly recall the impact of Title IX, which opened doors to greater career opportunities for women. I felt its direct influence as girls were permitted to participate in organized sports and wear pants to school for the first time. This shift, occurring in the early '70s, coincided with the beginning of my adolescence.

By the time I reached high school, girls were actively challenging the status quo on various levels, including sports and school dress codes. Our girls' basketball team garnered strong support, and seeing a girl wearing pants was no longer a novelty. To this day, the real potential of women and girls, especially Black women and girls, has not been realized. There are still too many "firsts" for us.

In 2022, the first Black woman, Ketanji Brown, became a Supreme Court Justice. Charlotte E. Ray was the first

Black woman to graduate from law school and be licensed to practice law in 1872. She was born in 1850 and died in 1911.

After a lengthy 152 years, history was finally made with the appointment of the first Black woman to the Supreme Court. While it's true that the barriers of the 19th century prevented women, particularly Black women, from pursuing legal education, such excuses grow increasingly hollow as we progress through the 21st century. This monumental achievement by Justice Brown not only shatters centuries-old ceilings of racial and gender discrimination but also marks a pivotal moment in our ongoing journey toward justice and equality.

Chapter 2: Childhood in Germany and Augusta, Georgia

As I reflect on my earliest memories, one moment stands out vividly against the backdrop of my childhood: my first international flight. It was when air travel held an air of sophistication, a time when dressing up for the occasion was as much a part of the journey as the destination itself. I remember the anticipation bubbling within me as I prepared for this monumental voyage and how my excitement was palpable.

Boarding that plane wasn't just about taking a flight; it was like opening the first page of a thrilling novel, the start of a lifelong love story with adventure. There was a rush of butterflies in my stomach as I embarked on a journey to a distant land waiting to be discovered.

Growing up as a military child, I quickly learned the art of adaptability, forging connections in fleeting moments, and bidding farewell with a bittersweet smile. Leaving behind familiar faces and places became a necessary ritual, yet it was one infused with a sense of wanderlust and curiosity that knew no bounds.

My first foray into the world beyond my homeland led me to the snowy landscapes of Germany, where I found myself immersed in a culture rich with history and tradition yet starkly contrasted by our status as Americans and as part of a small number of individuals of color amidst the snow-covered terrain. Living with a German host family during a school-based student exchange program opened my eyes to a captivating and unfamiliar world, sparking within me a desire to explore beyond the confines of my comfort zone.

On the military base where my family was stationed, I discovered a vibrant community teeming with opportunities for growth and exploration, from Teen Town escapades to school spirit that permeated every aspect of student life.

Education became not just a means to an end but a journey of self-discovery and empowerment. With teachers who were more than mere educators—they were mentors and champions of potential—I flourished academically and intellectually, guided by their unwavering support and dedication.

But amidst the excitement and adventure, my parents also instilled in me a sense of duty—a commitment to a relentless pursuit of knowledge, as evidenced by good grades. Their belief in the power of education shaped my worldview and laid the foundation for a future defined by achievement and purpose.

For me at that time, purpose meant getting heavily involved in my surroundings and school was my primary surrounding. I got to know most of the students and teachers at the school. I also asked a lot of questions about why things were done the way they were. All of that, coupled with my parents having me read books by Black authors, had me thinking seriously about what it means to be represented in your environment. At the school on base, there were not that many Black students and no Black teachers, although there were a few Black administrators.

I remember one particular year, as the school's annual Christmas gathering loomed, I wanted more than just twinkling lights on a tree, gifts, and jolly Santa. I wanted a Santa that looked like me.

"Why can't Santa be Black?" I demanded, my voice echoing through the classroom like a pebble skipping across water.

My classmates, hesitant at first, rallied around me. Together, a motley crew of kids shared this thought with our teacher, who encouraged us to tell the principal, and we did. To our surprise, not only did he listen, but he also did something about it. At the Christmas assembly, a Black administrator donned the Santa suit. He was the school's first Black Santa, and his presence meant a lot to me and signaled that we could make a difference and change things.

It was a victory, small but significant, a testament to the power of collective action.

After a four-year tour, I returned to the States for high school, settling in Augusta, Georgia, a city rich in history and marked by its ongoing struggles. Fort Gordon, now Fort Eisenhower, was the military base to which my dad was assigned, and it was only the second time our family had not lived in base housing. The first time was when my dad went to Vietnam. This time, my parents bought a house in a neighborhood very close to the base. Military people still surrounded us, but it was a different sense of freedom because I made friends in my neighborhood and my school with people who had no connection to the Army. All the houses didn't look alike, and there were no restrictions on putting nails in the walls, as well as all the other rules the military had that the family had to adhere to.

Returning to American soil, I faced the challenges of adolescence in a new cultural setting. With its unique customs, the Southern way of life felt unfamiliar and strangely familiar, blending the past with the present. However, this period wasn't just about moving geographically; it also sparked a profound change in how I saw the world.

My maternal relatives lived in Augusta and Martinez, another small town that was more rural than Augusta, which was considered metropolitan. For the first time, my grandparents, whom I only saw during summer break, lived minutes from us. We got to know them and spent more time with cousins and extended family.

What I liked most about that time was that our family would get together for cookouts and holiday dinners, and there would be eating, dancing, and storytelling. I learned a lot about my ancestry from those events. I had always been told how fearless and powerful my family was in the face of adversity. Having the opportunity to meet so many of the elders for the first time and hearing them talk about our ancestors who were born enslaved yet fought for their freedom, became landowners, contributed to the community, and stood up to white folks even when it was life-threatening began to shape my life.

One of my deepest regrets is that our family did not record those stories or formally interview the elders, who are all gone now. My oldest living relative, Frank Lampkin, died during COVID at the age of 90.

Meeting so many elders for the first time and hearing them talk about our ancestors instilled in me a deep sense of pride and resilience. This emphasis on family and heritage became even more pronounced after our time in Germany. Just as my return home shaped me, so did our time in Germany. It widened our perspectives, making us different from our peers.

Our experiences abroad influenced everything from our fashion choices to philosophical beliefs, shaping who we were and how we interacted with the world.

High school became a refuge where I could express myself freely, particularly through writing poetry. It was a way to explore my innermost thoughts and feelings, grappling with questions about who I was and my purpose. Despite the focus on self-discovery, my upbringing instilled a sense of practicality. My parents encouraged me to balance creative pursuits with practical goals, reminding me of the importance of responsibility. This meant finding a middle ground between artistic expression and real-world obligations. When I got into an advanced art class, my mom said, "That's great, but art is not a career."

In high school, I bought a chest from a store called Roses, where I worked. I cannot remember where I heard about Hope Chests. Maybe from my granny, Lucille Bussey Monon, who was always sharing wisdom with me in a quiet matter-of-fact way. What I heard was unmarried women used them to collect things for their marriage. Well, like so many things in my life, I can take a thing and turn it on its side and make it useful for my situation and my purposes.

Nope, that is not cultural appropriation; it's about a deep understanding that this world was not designed for a Black girl like me with my reality. That hope chest and how I used it was also a strong indicator, while I did not know it at the time, that I would not be a good daughter of the patriarchy. Guess what?

I am happy to say I have never been!!

That chest from the department store was, in so many ways, my hope chest. As a young Black girl, I filled it with hope for the future that I would live out my dreams and make a difference. I hoped that I would find a place for myself.

In my quest for knowledge and understanding, I found solace in books, expanding my understanding of the world and finding new perspectives. Apart from being able to skip chores, being involved in extracurricular activities also opened up a world of possibilities for me during my high school years. It was a time of great exploration—I tried my hand at various hobbies, eagerly took on extra class projects, and connected with a diverse array of people. One such project, a report on vegetarianism as a lifestyle, unexpectedly sparked a lifelong health journey. Though I didn't realize it then. I embraced vegetarianism two years later, at 18, when I left for college. Fast forward 47 years, and I'm still proudly a vegetarian.

I was heavily engaged in numerous clubs and activities, but my favorites were the art club, which I continue to enjoy painting, and the debate club. During the bicentennial celebrations, there were ample opportunities for debaters, and I had the honor of winning State in the category of Extemporaneous Speaking. Additionally, I held various officer positions on the student council, served as co-editor of the yearbook, and was a member of the esteemed Spartan Society—a select group of students recognized for their high GPA and exemplary extracurricular involvement, distinguishing them as leaders.

In my senior year, I was humbled to receive the Citizenship Award, the highest honor bestowed upon a student. Voted on by the teachers, this award recognized students who had significantly contributed to improving the school and enhancing student life throughout their high school years. I'll never forget the school assembly where I received the award; seeing my parents in the audience made the moment even more meaningful. It was a pivotal moment for me and my family—one that solidified my passion for community involvement and justified all the Saturdays I left before the chores were done!

High school was a transformative period that sharpened my leadership skills. While I didn't champion any social causes during those years, that didn't come until later when I entered college. I learned what it meant to lead people even when they were obstinate and how to be accountable because the buck stops with you when you are the leader.

Even if the breakdown wasn't your fault, it is yours to deal with, and people don't care about all the reasons. They just want results. Those were skills that came through hard lessons. And college brought even more lessons.

Chapter 3: College, Activism and Community Involvement

Growing up in a military family, I was accustomed to environments where people of different races interacted. President Truman's decision to abolish racial discrimination in the military in the late 1940s led to an increase in the number of Black people in the armed forces. The Vietnam War, in which my father served, marked the first time Black and white soldiers were not segregated. In my experience, most officers were white, while the majority of soldiers were Black. I vividly recall several instances of discrimination within the armed forces that left a lasting impact on me.

My father, Ceola Earl Barnhill, took it upon himself to teach Black history to fellow soldiers, I believe, as a response to discrimination and as a morale booster. Also, despite the diverse makeup of enlisted soldiers, there was a stark absence of Black officers or high-ranking enlisted men (E7-E9) during that time. The disparity in leadership positions underscored the systemic barriers faced by Black individuals within the military hierarchy.

Part of the culture, especially when my family was living overseas, was listening to music, especially music with a message. I learned a lot about resistance from the music my parents and other adults played in their homes and on the radio. There was a message in the music, and contrary to some opinions, I think there is still a message in music today. Back then, the soulful sounds of Curtis Mayfield served as a source of inspiration and solace amidst the racial tensions in the military.

I remember three songs in particular that people played often. The first, "Back to the World," was my introduction to Curtis Mayfield, and I remember it being played a lot during the Vietnam War. Although more Black soldiers died in the Vietnam War, especially in the early years of the war, and were disproportionately killed in later years, the song still expressed the soldiers' strong desire to make it home. The other two I heard a lot in Germany were "We Got to Have Peace" and "People Get Ready." Mayfield's music spoke to the struggles and resilience of the Black community, providing a sense of camaraderie and empowerment.

While the racism I witnessed deeply affected me, it also ignited a sense of determination and resilience. I observed Blacks within the military fighting tirelessly for their dignity and respect, serving as beacons of strength and perseverance, and coming home and finding second-class citizenship. However, it's worth noting that my observations were predominantly centered on Black men, as I don't recall encountering any Black women among the enlisted soldiers on the army base in Darmstadt, Germany, during our time there. Nevertheless, I am aware of the significant contributions of Black women in advocating for gender integration within the armed forces, particularly during World War II.

That desire to make a difference led me to engage in activism for the first time during middle school on the military base. While the details of this experience are described earlier in the book, I must say that the organizing skills I developed while rallying students around an issue have been invaluable throughout my activist journey.

I started my college journey in 1977 at Agnes Scott, a small women's college in Decatur, GA. It was there that I began my journey into activism. Transitioning to Agnes Scott, a predominantly white environment, I found myself among only two Black girls in the freshman class, with just ten Black students enrolled in total. Moreover, there were no Black faculty members. Recognizing this lack of diversity, the Black women at the college raised the issue, prompting Agnes Scott to take action. The college hired its first Black administrator in my second year, marking a significant step toward greater inclusivity. Today, black people are employed as teachers, administrators, and other staff. Black women's enrollment has increased significantly at Scott.

Over the years, I pondered various professions. In high school, I dreamed of becoming an actor, but my mom quickly dismissed that idea, emphasizing the need to secure financial stability in the real world. Aware of the precarious nature of acting careers, I shifted my focus to psychiatry, only to be deterred by reports of high suicide rates among psychiatrists.

Eventually, I found myself drawn to the legal profession, as others had remarked on my propensity to ask questions. I decided to pursue this path during my sophomore year at Scott. However, realizing that Agnes Scott didn't offer a pre-law major and feeling the need for a different environment to prepare for law school, I decided to transfer to Georgia State University (GSU) during the summer before my junior year.

At Georgia State University was where I planted the seeds of change in fertile ground.

While there wasn't a pre-law major at GSU, the Political Science Department provided a strong foundation for law school preparation, particularly through its quasi-Moot Court program run by one of the professors and its emphasis on engagement with the state legislature. The affordability of in-state tuition at GSU, coupled with the realization that I'd need to start covering my expenses since I was no longer on scholarship, made the decision even more appealing.

However, transitioning to GSU meant facing new challenges. Those changes ranged from moving from a residential college to a commuter school. Without on-campus dorms at the time, I had to find employment and secure housing off-campus. Fortunately, I connected with a high school classmate already attending GSU, and we became roommates, marking the beginning of my journey into adulthood.

My first year at GSU was hard socially. When I lived on campus at Scott, I had a ready-made community. I knew the women who lived in the dorm room next door not just because I was a Resident Assistant (RA) but because I was a friendly person. I made it a point to get to know students in other dorms on campus. Once I moved into an apartment. I rarely saw the people who lived next door. Or if I did see them, they were getting in their cars, and I was heading to the bus stop. I realized later that I was trying to find "my people" – those individuals and groups with whom I felt comfortable and had commonalities.

As I mentor younger people, I encourage them to find their people and build strong and lasting relationships with them so that they have a support system. Back then, I was not sure how to connect with people, so I decided to get involved first in my local community and then at GSU.

In the late 1970s—early 1980s, Atlanta was alive with energy. Maynard Jackson, the first Black mayor, created the Neighborhood Planning (NPU) system, which is still in place today, and allowed local residents to give input into what was happening in their community. Before a new business could enter a residential or mixed-use area, it had to attend a community meeting to talk with the residents and get their input. The hope was always that the residents would highly recommend your business; even if they didn't, it did not mean a business could not get approval from the city government.

I started attending the NPU meetings for my community, now called Old Fourth Ward and met people who cared about what was happening in the city and in their neighborhood. I saw residents with deep roots in the community talking about neighborhood revitalization and limiting the commercial businesses that encroached on the neighborhood or outsiders who bought up property and flipped it. Today, in Atlanta, like in communities around the country, the same conversation we began in the 70s is still being held.

During that time, my NPU president was a GSU student who was married and working. At NPU meetings, he introduced me to other GSU students in the community. Like me and all the other students, they came to campus to attend classes and then left for work so my efforts to connect in the community worked, but not at college.

Part of me longed for a sense of connection and school spirit, but I wasn't sure how to fill the void. I thought about joining a sorority. I loved the fact that the Deltas and AKAs on campus focused on volunteering and community service. Still, my work schedule, limited finances, and personality didn't make sororities a fit for me. So, I turned to the student clubs, and while I found some interesting ones, I did not find a fit for me.

I remember GSU, at that time, had a Black student organization, and I began attending some of their events and meeting other students. At one of their events, I met Victor Brown, the fellow student who co-founded the NAACP College chapter at Georgia State, which proved to be a turning point. It was the first time I realized I liked creating new things and bringing ideas to the marketplace. Since then, I have started many organizations, groups, and collaborations.

Victor's family had a long history of NAACP involvement, with his mother being active in the Atlanta chapter. As a youth, he had already been involved in building his leadership and activism skills. While I was new to the NAACP structure of college chapters, I believed in its mission at that time to ensure the political and educational equality of minority group citizens of the United States and eliminate racial prejudice.

Today, the NAACP has an expanded mission[3] to achieve equity, political rights, and social inclusion by advancing policies and practices that expand human and civil rights, eliminate discrimination, and accelerate the well-being, education, and economic security of Black people and all persons of color.

In 2021, the GSU NAACP college chapter was selected nationally as the best college chapter. I don't know where Victor is, but I hope he knows that the work we did decades ago planted seeds that have grown into a mighty student tree of activists on GSU's campus.

While the GSU NAACP was working on issues of racism, there were rumblings in the city around the plight of young Black children. Camille Bell, the mother of Yusef Bell, was speaking out and challenging the city to care about Black children who the police seemed not to be concerned about. It was during this time that the "Missing and Murdered

---

[3] https://naacp.org/about/mission-vision#:~:text=Our%20mission%20is%20to%20achieve,and%20all%20persons%20of%20color.

Children"[4] crisis gripped Atlanta. From 1979 to 1981, there were about 29 murders in the Atlanta area that appeared to be linked. Most of the victims were boys, and all of them were black. The majority were young — and some were even children. The community dubbed the killing spree the Atlanta Child Murders.

A mysterious killer terrorized Black communities in Atlanta. One by one, Black children and young adults were being kidnapped and turning up dead days or weeks later[5]. Across the city, groups were forming into search parties that would go to wooded areas in the vicinity of where victims were found to search for bodies. At Georgia State University, students were organizing as well, and on Saturday mornings, we ventured into the city's underbelly, searching for any trace of the vanished.

Though our efforts yielded no immediate answers, the experience left an indelible mark, further solidifying my decision to pursue law school and advocate for justice on a larger scale.

These formative years shaped the person I am today. The reverberations of unfairness still echo in me, now intertwined with a strong urge to act. Every stage of my life, from childhood to university, has molded me into the person I am today, a relentless defender of fairness and equal rights.

---

[4] https://allthatsinteresting.com/wayne-williams#:~:text=From%201979%20to%201981%2C%20there,spree%20the%20Atlanta%20Child%20Murders.

[5] https://allthatsinteresting.com/atlanta-child-murders

Throughout the book, I'll share my experiences and what drove me to become involved in the community. Born in 1959, I heard about the activism of that era and saw it on the news, but I wasn't directly involved in protesting or experiencing jail time like some of my predecessors. I felt I was born too late.

Regardless of the era, looking back on the road that led me here, I am thankful for the trials that ignited my dedication and reinforced my determination to effect change.

Chapter 4: Picking the Path Less Traveled

Choosing a law school wasn't easy for me. Unlike many peers, I didn't have family members to guide me. While members of my family had college degrees, no one had an advanced degree or had been to law school. Education was at the top of the adults' minds for young people in my family, so they spurred me on, but no one could tell me what to expect or base my decision on.

My relative on my mother's side, Julia Johnson, whom we called Aunt Julia, was our stalwart. She was an educator who went on to work toward her Master's. The family was so proud of her. Not only did she have a strong mind, but she also had a gentle spirit. Her immediate family affectionately called her "Ma Dear," a derivation of Mother Dear and a very southern term of endearment.

Aunt Julia was one of my family's matriarchs and a beautiful example of a tough mind and a tender heart.

I applied to six schools, and the University of Denver was one of them. They accepted me early and gave me a scholarship, so I thought I was set. I was near family and had a free ride.

My decision to attend law school in Denver was largely influenced by a cousin, Delmar Davis, who lived there. He was an entrepreneur, and his achievements have always inspired me. He was an active part of our family while growing up, so I thought, let me go to a city where someone I know will support me and, if needed, feed me. He and his wife, Linda, were always encouraging, and they had a strong family foundation, so that also spoke to me.

I came from a working-class family, and my parents were clear about two things: education is the way up, and you will need scholarships to get your degree. After leaving Agnes Scott and working my way through GSU, where money for school was an issue, I knew that unless I got a scholarship, I could not go. I was determined to go to law school, so I thought I had just grasped the brass ring when I was accepted to the University of Denver.

Like the chest I filled up in high school, I did the same for law school. I bought a chest from Sears. I have always been an "A" type personality and made lists. There is something so satisfying about crossing things off the list. I am an ENFJ on the Myers Briggs Type Indicator (MBTI. I made my list and started putting everything I thought I would need in it, too. Other than when we lived in Germany, I had never lived in a cold climate, so I started filling the trunk I bought with sweaters and heavy socks to keep me warm.

I was set on attending law school in Denver, but fate had other plans. I checked a box on the LSAT that said to send my scores to other schools interested in minority students with my LSAT score and GPA. As I think back, being a risk-taker, being willing to take a chance, and wanting more has always been part of my DNA. When I checked the box, I didn't think it would change anything, but it did - it changed everything.

I received an irresistible offer from the University of Texas (UT). The University of Denver offered me a scholarship that covered all my expenses, but the difference was that UT was ranked among the top 10 law schools in the country at that time. That was a big deal. I said yes immediately.

When I arrived in Austin, I joined the Black Law Students Association (BLSA), which everyone called BALSA. This group was pivotal, not just for the sense of community it offered, but because it was deeply involved in advocacy and legal challenges that were beginning to shape my view of what law could do in the world.

One of our major challenges was affirmative action policies, which faced significant legal scrutiny at the time. The federal government even stepped in to investigate and interview students. In 2023, the Bakke case was finally overturned. This exposure to the intersection of law and civil rights issues began to steer my career aspirations.

My leadership role as the BALSA President placed me at the forefront of significant discussions and actions affecting the law school's approach to critical issues like diversity and inclusion. I proudly served on the Admissions Committee. This experience, which was both demanding and fulfilling, strengthened my dedication to utilizing the legal system as a tool for social justice.

Alongside another student, Dola Young, we created what I'll call a Black Law Student Orientation Weekend, though it was much more than that.

Recognizing that many of us, especially Black and Latinx students, were the first in our families to attend law school, we understood there were cultural and practical nuances that weren't familiar to us, unlike our white peers, many of whom grew up around lawyers and had at least a rudimentary understanding of the legal field. Dwight Thomas was the first lawyer I met and extensively talked with about a legal career. I met him during my senior year in college. He is still active in the legal community.

The orientation weekend was designed to demystify the law school experience. We contacted incoming Black law students, inviting them to arrive early. For those who couldn't move into their apartments immediately, we arranged for them to stay with fellow students if they could not afford a hotel. During the orientation, we explained essential concepts and terms like what a 'hornbook' is, how to participate in study groups, and the general culture of law school, which might not be obvious to someone new.

We also focused on building a community. When the official school orientation started a week later, these students had a network, foundational knowledge, and a sense of belonging. The success of this program inspired the Latino Association at the school to start a similar initiative the following year. It is one of the things I am most proud of during my law school career.

We didn't stop at providing information; we gathered and distributed resources. We recognized the financial strain many students faced, even those on full scholarships like me, so we collected used law books and materials from upper-class students. These were organized into large binders and given to new students, ensuring they had the necessary materials without the financial burden.

The mentorship aspect was also vital. We paired new students with upper-class students who served as mentors, helping them navigate the unique culture of our law school. Understanding the specific culture of your institution can make or break your law school experience.

This effort to build a supportive community was about more than just succeeding academically; it was about ensuring everyone could thrive in an environment that was unusual and unique to many of us. I love that part about building community within a neighborhood, a law school, or anywhere in the world.

What matters the most is people who care with true intentions and are ready to invest in your success. This project was one of the most fulfilling parts of my law school experience, and looking back, I realize how foundational it was not just for me but for all those who came after us.

While in law school, I realized how these experiences, from my initial decision to attend, my role in student organizations, and my firsthand encounters with systemic inequalities, have shaped my approach to law and justice.

My journey through law school was about acquiring knowledge and learning to apply that knowledge in ways that aligned with my deeper values of equity and community advocacy.

During my second year, I participated in a legal clinic that was a turning point. I worked on the case of a Black man who was convicted of a robbery and murder, and his co-conspirator, who was white, was able to afford a lawyer. The sentences these two men got were very different. The Black man got the death penalty, and the white man got a long prison sentence. That case and others highlighted the inequalities in the criminal justice system.

The disparity in terms of treatment and sentencing of Black defendants makes it painfully clear that the system is flawed, racially-biased, and overwhelmingly stacked against those who come from impoverished backgrounds, are people of color, and lack the significant financial means to afford proper representation. I've met some dedicated public defenders throughout my career, but even the best are stretched thin, underpaid, and overburdened.

It also ignited my resolve to focus on social justice after graduation. Despite the attractive allure of oil and gas law, a significant sector in Texas, I chose instead to return to the South and work on issues like the death penalty and prison conditions.

This realization steered me toward my first legal job in a nonprofit focused solely on death penalty cases in the Deep South. However, I didn't stay long with that group. I moved on to another legal nonprofit group that also did death penalty work in Georgia and other southern states, where I continued to work on death penalty cases.

In 1985, the top four states with death row prisoners were Florida, Texas, California, and Georgia, and black people were disproportionately represented.[6]

Fast forward 39 years to 2024, and Black people are still disproportionately represented in the death penalty. Black people made up about 41% of death row inmates while only making up about 13% of the U.S. population.[7]

While the law is a powerful tool for change, it must be utilized justly and equitably. The legal system needs more than reform; it requires a complete overhaul to truly serve justice.

This conviction drives my commitment to my work and advocacy for those most marginalized by our current system.

More and more people and organizations are using the term "criminal legal system" to describe policing, prosecution, courts, and corrections in the United States. Accuracy in language matters, and these systems do not deliver justice, nor have they ever.[8]

---

[6] https://bjs.ojp.gov/content/pub/pdf/cp85.pdf

[7] NACDL - Race and the death penalty. (n.d.). NACDL - National Association of Criminal Defense Lawyers. https://www.nacdl.org/Content/Race-and-the-Death-Penalty#:~:text=Disparities%20in%20the%20makeup%20of,(American%20Progress%2C%202019)

[8] Bryant, Erica. "Why We Say "Criminal Legal System," Not "Criminal Justice System."" Vera Institute of Justice, 1 Dec. 2021, www.vera.org/news/why-we-say-criminal-legal-system-not-criminal-justice-system.

Recognizing this reality, I refer to it not as the criminal justice system but simply as the criminal legal system because this echoes the sentiments of many of those with lived experiences with the system and activists who recognize its profound imperfections.

My experiences fueled my determination to serve and fight against this systemic injustice, but the inequities also made me decide to leave the practice of law.

I am particularly proud of and happy to know Tiffany Williams Roberts, an attorney at the Southern Center for Human Rights and Director of Public Policy. Before her assuming this role, Marissa Dodson, who died prematurely in 2021 and was a member of the Advisory Board of Foreverfamily, the agency I founded, held that position. These two powerhouse Black women worked together and have been at the forefront in Georgia and nationally, calling for reform.

I do not believe the law is the answer. Yes, the law is part of the answer, but the answer is we, the people, working to form a more perfect union. As a Black lawyer, I strove to be a light source for those entangled in this flawed and unjust system. But I was pretty clear: more work must be done so people never get into the criminal legal system.

I have experienced our system being deeply engulfed by racism and white supremacy, and it has disproportionately failed people of color and the impoverished. Whether Black, brown, or white, you are less likely to receive fair treatment or adequate representation if you lack financial resources.

This ugly reality underscores a broader truth: our society privileges those with means, money, and status, which is fundamentally unjust. We must advocate for change.

Growing up, and even during my travels to places like Germany, I observed significant ethnocentrism, a belief that one's culture is superior. This perspective was both eye-opening and disheartening. I realized how important it is to do our personal, internal work, which involves examining our prejudices, bias, internalized oppression, and trauma and acquiring information to educate ourselves, not expecting others to do that. Then couple that interior work with outer work in the form of advocacy to combat ignorance and promote a broader understanding of justice and equity.

We should all have a better understanding of our own culture and the history of what shaped it, as well as the cultures of others, which could result in more informed and empathic decisions for a better, more just world.

Chapter 5: Fighting Injustice in the Legal System

As I transitioned from the educational realm into the professional world, my resolve to fight against systemic injustices, particularly in the sphere of the death penalty and prison conditions, became more pronounced. My years in law school in Texas and the poignant reminder of cases where the outcomes were too influenced by race and resources had deeply affected me. It was an awakening to the grim realities many faced within the justice system—an area that demanded courage and compassion.

After graduating, I was determined to work directly on issues that resonated with my core values. I began searching for opportunities aligned with my commitment to justice reform, particularly those involving the death penalty. This search led me back to Atlanta, where I interviewed with various legal groups dedicated to this cause.

My journey to becoming fully credentialed as a lawyer was a personal battle. I faced significant challenges in passing the bar exam. I am not a naturally gifted test-taker, and I failed multiple attempts before I finally passed the bar. This struggle, while frustrating, reinforced my resolve to persist in this field—it was a constant reminder of the barriers that often discourage talented individuals from pursuing or continuing in legal careers, particularly those from non-traditional backgrounds.

I worked for a short time with one legal group working on the death penalty and transitioned to another nonprofit, which also focused on the death penalty and prison condition cases. Here, I found my footing. Over the next three to four years, I immersed myself in the work, which was grueling yet gratifying. Our team was small, but our resolve to make a significant impact was immense. We tackled each case with a dual approach: advocating for the prisoners and striving to reform the systems perpetuating their suffering. This period was about planting the seeds of broader systemic change.

The experience was eye-opening. It illustrated the sheer magnitude of disparity and the often-overlooked human stories behind each case. Our goal was to challenge and ultimately transform the punitive practices that had long been accepted as the norm. Each case was a battle in the larger war against a system fraught with inequities.

One of the pivotal cases that profoundly impacted my commitment was a women's prison conditions case in Alabama. This case stood out not only because of its complexity but also due to the glaring inequalities it highlighted within the system. We sued the state of Alabama and the Department of Corrections based on issues of parity for women prisoners. The men had access to various educational and vocational programs. At the same time, the only class available to women was cosmetology—a field they couldn't even legally enter upon release due to licensing restrictions for felons. This disparity was not just an oversight; it was a systemic failure, perpetuating a cycle of disadvantage and discrimination.

Working alongside a seasoned woman lawyer in our office, Christine Freeman, who brought years of experience and sharp acumen to our team, was enlightening. Her mentorship was central to my growth as a legal professional. Our collaboration on this case challenged the status quo and pushed for tangible changes in the prison system, aiming to ensure equitable treatment and opportunities for all inmates, regardless of gender.

Throughout this period, my perspective on law and justice continued to evolve. It wasn't merely about winning cases; it was about understanding the broader impact of our work on the lives of individuals and on society as a whole. This realization underscored the importance of our efforts and the need for sustained advocacy and reform.

During my tenure focusing on prison conditions for women in the southern states, including Alabama and Louisiana, I confronted the stark realities these prisoners faced daily. Women, though only constituting about 6% of the prison population, were significantly underserved and overlooked in terms of educational and vocational opportunities. This demographic disparity was not just a statistic; it was a reflection of a broader systemic indifference toward the unique needs and rights of female prisoners.

The conditions of confinement were often dire, with limited resources allocated to anything beyond the bare necessities. Most notably, the disproportionate budget that was allocated for healthcare, specifically for gynecological issues, was both a necessity and a reminder of the unique health challenges women face, which are exacerbated in prison environments. Despite this, there was a glaring lack of comprehensive educational programs that could provide these women with skills and knowledge applicable outside the prison walls.

One particularly striking aspect was the discovery that many courses, such as cosmetology, were ironically irrelevant in the real world due to licensing restrictions for felons. This not only limited their reintegration prospects but also underscored the cyclic nature of challenges they faced—from incarceration to reentry into society.

The stories of these women were not just narratives of confinement; they were tales of systemic neglect and missed opportunities for rehabilitation and growth. Through our legal challenges, we sought to address these immediate disparities and highlight and question the long-standing policies that perpetuated such conditions.

Our work helped to bring these issues to the forefront, contributing to the growing awareness of the need for tailored rehabilitative and educational programs for women in prison.

These legal battles were not just professional obligations; they were deeply personal. Each case was a mosaic of individual lives impacted by a system that too often failed to recognize their humanity. These women, whose stories I carried with me, enriched my understanding of justice and the profound responsibility of those who wield the law as a tool of enforcement and an instrument of change.

Diving deeper into the reasons behind the incarceration of women, it's crucial to understand the nature of the crimes for which they were often imprisoned. One poignant example I encountered during my work was a woman sentenced to five years for writing $500 worth of bad checks to grocery stores. Unable to make restitution, she found herself caught in the punitive grasp of the legal system. This scenario was not unique but rather emblematic of a broader pattern of "economic crimes" that disproportionately affected women.

These economic crimes typically included acts like shoplifting, credit card fraud, and welfare fraud—crimes often driven by desperation and the need to provide for their families. As societal pressures mounted, these women, many of whom were primary caregivers, resorted to whatever means necessary to care for their loved ones.

Over time, the escalation of the drug crisis further complicated the landscape, leading to an increase in women incarcerated for drug-related offenses. Yet, the narrative that emerged was not one of hardened criminals but of individuals pushed to the margins of society, grappling with systemic failures that offered few alternatives.

The nature of crimes for which women were incarcerated starkly contrasted with those of their male counterparts. While men were more frequently imprisoned for violent crimes such as robbery and murder, women were overwhelmingly represented in categories that involved non-violent, survival-driven offenses. This disparity speaks volumes about the social and economic dynamics that influence criminal behavior and the subsequent legal repercussions.

This understanding sheds light on the systemic biases embedded within the legal system. It raises poignant questions about the role of justice in addressing not just the act of crime but the underlying societal conditions that catalyze these acts. As the percentage of women in prison rose from 6% to 20% during the early years of my career, it became increasingly clear that addressing these issues required a multifaceted approach—one that considered the socio-economic drivers of crime and aimed at rehabilitative, rather than purely punitive, solutions.

The critical examination of disparities and flaws in the criminal legal system reveals a landscape riddled with systemic issues that are often overlooked or tolerated. It's a complex tapestry of sexism, racial injustice, and deep-seated biases that permeate every level of the legal framework.

Sexism within the legal system is not just a peripheral issue; it is ingrained and pervasive. Women in the system face not only legal battles but also stigmatized battles against deeply entrenched stereotypes. The old tactics of undermining women's achievements by attributing their success to 'favors' rather than merit is an egregious reflection of the misogyny still prevalent in many sectors, including law. This is not merely an injustice; it's a systemic strategy to delegitimize and disempower.

Addressing the elephant in the room, the racial injustices that persist, particularly in Southern states, is crucial. My commitment to practicing law in the South was driven by an acute awareness of the ongoing struggles and the need for voices advocating for change. A deep belief in the transformative potential of this region shaped my journey. Despite their beauty and charm, states like Alabama, Georgia, Louisiana, and Mississippi harbor some of the most glaring examples of legal and societal inequities.

However, my experiences made me realize that the law alone is not the panacea for these deep-rooted issues. The people—our communities—are the true answer. This realization led to a pivotal shift in my career path from being purely a lawyer to becoming an activist, organizer, social justice advocate, and writer. By engaging at the grassroots level, I could enact changes that the legal system alone could not achieve.

The narrative that often dominates discussions about criminal justice focuses on punitive measures rather than preventative ones. It's not enough to address issues after they've escalated to the point of incarceration. We need proactive solutions that address the root causes— educational disparities, economic inequities, and lack of community resources—that lead individuals down these paths in the first place.

Furthermore, the journey of reform is not just about rectifying visible injustices but also about challenging the underlying assumptions and biases, unconscious or not, that perpetuate these systemic flaws. From the codes and practices within the police force to the politicians who often ignore these issues for electoral gains, the entire spectrum of the justice system requires a fundamental overhaul that leads to a better justice system.

As a society, we must peel back the layers of surface-level perceptions and delve into the complexities that define real life. Growing up, I witnessed both white privilege and the gradual unveiling of systemic injustices that challenged my initial perceptions about law and justice. This journey of awakening is not unique to me but is a path that many must traverse to truly understand and engage with the intricacies of justice.

Although the task ahead is daunting, it is not insurmountable. With a collective effort and a shift in societal and legal priorities, we can begin to mend the broken systems that fail so many. Our efforts must be concerted and persistent, aiming not just to change laws but to transform the cultural and societal structures that underpin these legal systems. This is the only way to ensure a just society where everyone can find their rightful place without being marred by past convictions or systemic barriers.

The early years of my career were intense and fulfilling, though they also taught me that while the law is a critical tool for change, it is not the sole answer. True change requires a broader societal movement toward justice, with the law being one of many tools leveraged in this battle.

After four years, I picked up another tool called direct service, which I will talk about later in the book.

Chapter 6: Balancing Personal and Professional Life

The challenge of balancing activism with maintaining personal relationships often felt like navigating a landscape dotted with both landmines and treasures. My professional life was relentlessly demanding, deeply entwined with the often-grim realities of the prison industrial complex and the personal turmoil of families ensnared within it. This part of my life demanded not only my time but also an emotional depth that could be all-consuming.

Despite the gravity of my work, I knew the importance of preserving a semblance of balance. My personal life needed to be a refuge where I could replenish the emotional reserves that my activism depleted. Cultivating nurturing and supportive relationships was essential, yet this was easier said than done.

My approach to personal relationships, especially romantic ones, was deliberate and introspective. This wasn't about finding someone who could cheer from the sidelines but someone who genuinely understood the weight of my commitments and shared my fundamental passions.

In the realm of friendships, I embraced connections that offered both solace and laughter. The men and women in my life provided a tapestry of support that was as varied as it was vibrant. These people reminded me that even when dedicated to serious causes, life also needed unguarded joy and relaxation moments.

Navigating these relationships required a keen sense of self-awareness. I had to recognize when to step back and nurture my well-being. There were times when the boundary between my professional and personal life blurred, creating tensions that were neither easy nor comfortable to address. In these moments, I learned the importance of clear communication and the art of saying no—a skill just as vital as any other in maintaining one's mental health and emotional well-being.

Additionally, my spiritual life played a crucial role in managing these dual aspects of my life. Through faith, I often found the strength to continue and the clarity to see when my reserves ran low. Prayer and reflection provided a grounding force, helping me recalibrate and ensure that I gave to myself and others.

The interplay between my personal faith and professional endeavors also brought unique challenges. Sometimes, the path I felt called to walk was lonely and misunderstood by those I dated or considered friends. Yet, these experiences taught me the value of resilience and the importance of being anchored in one's convictions.

The challenge is not simply about maintaining a balance but actively crafting a life where personal fulfillment and professional effectiveness coexist. It's about allowing each to inform and enrich the other, creating a dynamic where personal happiness and professional dedication are not at odds but in harmony.

Engaging in activism while fostering meaningful personal relationships is an intricate dance that requires rhythm, and patience. It's a path that continues to unfold, each step teaching me more about myself and how I relate to the world around me. As I navigate this journey, I remain committed to the belief that personal peace is just as crucial as professional achievement and that one can fuel the other.

My journey has been both enlightening and liberating. The relationships I've cultivated, particularly with my female friends, have been pivotal in my personal growth and emotional resilience. Women have a unique way of providing profound and empowering support through shared experiences and unspoken understandings.

The camaraderie and solidarity I found in my friendships with women have been nothing short of a lifeline. These relationships are built on mutual respect, empathy, and an innate understanding that often goes beyond words. We share the triumphs and tribulations not just as friends but as confidants and sisters-in-arms in our various personal and professional battles.

As for romantic relationships, I have loved deeply and appreciate the value found in sharing my life with another. I am grateful that relationships have taught me invaluable lessons about love, compromise, shared values, and emotional compatibility. They have also taught me the importance of recognizing when a relationship does not serve my well-being and that the primary declaration in a relationship is self-respect and an affirmation of my commitment to peace and happiness.

One pivotal lesson I learned from therapy is the importance of harmony between personal and professional life.

You cannot allow turmoil in one area to unsettle the other; peace must be the foundation upon which both stand. This understanding has guided me in setting boundaries that protect this peace, ensuring that the chaos of my professional world does not disrupt the sanctuary I've built in my personal life.

The concept of self-care has evolved for me over the years. It began with the basic understanding of taking time for myself but has deepened into a more holistic approach that encompasses emotional, mental, and spiritual well-being. It means saying no when necessary, prioritizing my needs, and recognizing the signs of burnout before they take hold. It also means engaging in activities that replenish my spirit and connect me to my passions outside of work, whether a quiet afternoon with a book, a lively dinner with friends, or a solitary walk in nature.

Moreover, wellness is also about the community you build around you. It's about fostering environments, both at work and home, that are supportive and enriching. This enhances my ability to give to others and ensures that I am supported. My home is my retreat, where I can reflect and recharge away from the demands of my advocacy work. It reflects all the parts of me. It is filled with textiles, artifacts, and items that my friends and I have gotten on trips to Africa, as well as artwork that speaks to my Black experience in the U.S.

It is a space filled with warmth, laughter, and love, decorated with reminders of the many journeys I have undertaken, literally and metaphorically.

For me, romantic and platonic relationships have been about connecting to and valuing those who bring positivity, growth, and peace into my life and inspire me to reciprocate in kind. The people we surround ourselves with—lovers, friends, family, colleagues—play pivotal roles in our lives. They influence our outlook, impact our decisions, and shape our experiences. Thus, choosing people who 'walk us home'—those who provide comfort, understanding, and encouragement—is crucial.

Communication plays a key role in fostering these relationships. It's about expressing needs clearly and listening actively, creating a dialogue that respects boundaries and embraces individual aspirations. Healthy relationships are characterized by open conversations where both parties feel heard and valued, conflicts are navigated with care, and resolutions are reached with mutual respect.

In my own journey, the emphasis on cultivating such relationships has been transformative. It has allowed me to maintain a sense of peace amidst the chaos of professional demands. This peace is not merely the absence of conflict but the presence of restorative connections that recharge and inspire. These relationships are the sanctuaries that provide respite from the storms, the safe harbors where I can dock my boat in turbulent seas.

The essence of these connections lies in the joy and support they provide and in their capacity to foster a deeper understanding of myself and the world around me. They teach me love, compromise, resilience, and the beauty of shared experiences. They remind me that while my professional endeavors may be fulfilling, the relationships I nurture hold the keys to my personal satisfaction and emotional well-being.

I became single again in the late -90s, which afforded me unique flexibility in my life—a freedom I channeled into my activism. Not having children to care for gave me more time and energy to dedicate to justice work, a cause that demands commitment and a deep emotional and temporal investment.

Maintaining this balance—where activism does not overshadow personal life and vice versa—has been a delicate endeavor. My personal life remains just that: personal. It's a sacred space, cherished and protected, where I find comfort and rejuvenation away from the public eye of my professional world. This privacy has allowed me to enjoy genuine relationships without the pressure of public scrutiny, preserving the purity of these personal interactions.

The notion of balance might suggest an equal distribution of time and energy, but it's about the quality of engagement in each aspect of life. My activism, while consuming, has never fully eclipsed my personal experiences. Instead, they have enriched it. My nurtured relationships have provided emotional sustenance, enhancing my resilience and perspective.

In discussing these personal decisions, I hope to illuminate the complexities of life choices and their implications on our broader commitments.

My personal and professional experiences have been significantly shaped by my not having children, allowing me to devote considerable energy to my nonprofit work. This has afforded me a unique perspective on how personal relationships and family commitments intersect with professional and activist endeavors.

I profoundly respect those, particularly women, who manage the dual responsibilities of parenting and activism. These remarkable individuals navigate a complex dynamic that I have observed but have not personally experienced. Their ability to juggle these demanding roles with grace and efficacy is inspiring. The strength required to manage a household, raise children, and contribute passionately to a cause is immense and deserves acknowledgment.

I have had the privilege through the nonprofit I started to engage with over 45,000 children. I often think of the thousands of children impacted by my nonprofit as "my children" in a broader sense. Each interaction with these young individuals has informed my understanding of the impact one can make, reinforcing the significance of my work and the personal fulfillment it brings.

I have had flexibility and intensity in my professional pursuits that might have been more challenging if I were a parent. The freedom to pour myself into my work without the same level of domestic responsibilities as a parent has enabled me to reach out to the community in expansive ways.

Most of the men I know doing movement work put their work front and center, as do women in the movement. Often, the responsibilities men and women face in the movement are different. Men often have wives or supportive partners who co-parent with them. I do want to lift up male activists who equally share family responsibilities. Their commitment to both their movement work and their roles at home is a testament to the possibility of balance and shared responsibilities, challenging the traditional norms that often place the bulk of family duties on women.

It's important to address and dismantle some pervasive stereotypes that not only misrepresent but also undermine the richness of relationships within the Black community.

Throughout my life, I have been privileged to form bonds with Black men who defy the negative stereotypes often perpetuated by both media and societal narratives. Contrary to the harmful clichés, my experiences with Black men have been overwhelmingly positive, characterized by respect, integrity, and mutual support. These romantic and platonic relationships have shaped my understanding and appreciation of connecting deeply with another person.

They have also reminded me that there is a dominant narrative in this country whose roots are steeped deeply in white supremacy that is deadly and seeks to undermine the foundation of powerful life-affirming relationships. Dominant narratives, sometimes called dominant cultural narratives, are frequently repeated stories shared in society through various social and cultural institutions.

A very pervasive and destructive one is that Black men and women are at odds and don't find value in each other. Nothing could be further than the truth. Black love in all its forms is Black wealth.

This narrative—of mutual respect and collective work — counters the often one-dimensional portrayal of Black relationships in the public sphere. It's crucial to highlight that the bond between Black men and women is built on a foundation of deep affection and shared aspirations, contrary to the frequently depicted discord and dysfunction.

Connecting to Black men, whether lovers or friends, has enriched my personal and professional life. It has provided insights into the reality that Black people love each other and want a world where Black love is celebrated and allowed to flourish without the labels and erroneous judgments that the dominant group has placed on it.

Personal relationships—whether they are romantic partnerships, friendships, or bonds with colleagues in the movement—play a crucial role in sustaining activists. They provide the emotional nourishment necessary to continue the often-draining work of social change. These relationships are the backbone of resilience, offering a network of support that rejuvenates the spirit and motivates continued effort.

In understanding these dynamics, my respect deepens for those who balance family and activism and for all who navigate the complex interplay of personal commitments and professional passions. Each story within the movement is a unique blend of sacrifice, love, and dedication, highlighting the diverse ways individuals contribute to and draw strength from their personal and professional communities.

I've come to understand that love is not merely a private affair of the heart but a potent force that energizes and sustains my activism. It is the most powerful force in the universe, transforming personal lives and societal structures. This belief in the transformative power of love underpins my personal relationships and my professional ethos as an activist. Love drives my passion for justice and equity, and it is this passion that has shaped my life's work.

In reflecting on the interplay between love and activism, it becomes evident that the power of love extends far beyond the romantic sphere. It infuses the relationships within our communities, bolsters our resilience, and empowers us to make impactful choices.

Counter-narratives are just that- narratives that are the opposite of what white supremacy says. They are stories that detail the experiences and perspectives of those historically oppressed, excluded, or silenced in various settings. In her poem Nikki Rose, Nikki Giovanni crafts a powerful counternarrative.[9]

Nikki-Rosa

By Nikki Giovanni

Childhood remembrances are always a drag

If you're Black

You always remember things like living in Woodlawn

With no inside toilet

And if you become famous or something

They never talk about how happy you were to have

Your mother

All to yourself and

How good the water felt when you got your bath

From one of those

Big tubs that folk in Chicago barbecue in

And somehow, when you talk about home

It never gets across how much you

Understood their feelings

As the whole family attended meetings about Hollydale

---

[9] Nikki Giovanni, "Nikki-Rosa" from *Black Feeling, Black Talk, Black Judgment.* Copyright © 1968, 1970 by Nikki Giovanni. Used with the permission of HarperCollins Publishers. Source: *The Collected Poetry of Nikki Giovanni* (2003)

And even though you remember

Your biographers never understand

Your father's pain as he sells his stock

And another dream goes

And though you're poor, it isn't poverty that

Concerns you

And though they fought a lot

It isn't your father's drinking that makes any difference

But only that everybody is together and you

And your sister, have happy birthdays and very good

Christmases

And I really hope no white person ever has cause

To write about me

Because they never understand

Black love is Black wealth, and they'll

Probably talk about my hard childhood

And never understand that

All the while I was quite happy

Chapter 7: Establishing a Nonprofit and Finding Purpose

In my late twenties, a different career path emerged—one that was less about following well-trodden legal pathways and more about carving a new trail that could lead to broader societal change. At 28, I started to feel a pull towards something transcending the confines of conventional legal practice.

This period marked a time of deeply personal reflection. I realized that law was a powerful tool, yet it was not the complete solution to the social injustices I was passionate about addressing. It could build the framework for a fair society, but it was not enough to heal the deeper wounds of exclusion and inequality. My faith, a background melody throughout my life, began to swell into a guiding force during this time.

It was a sermon one Sunday at church that sparked a transformative thought. The pastor spoke of two paths: living within God's "permissible will"—a safe and decent life, doing right by society's standards—and striving for God's "perfect will," which promised a challenging but impactful journey. This message struck a chord, resonating deeply with my yearning to do more meaningful work.

Spurred by that sermon and my personal growth journey as a church elder, I questioned, probed, and sought clarity on how to serve God's will and my community best. This dialogue with God wasn't about seeking signs for personal gain but about understanding where I could most effectively make a real difference for the kingdom of God.

The two cases the office filed in the Deep South over parity and conditions of confinement and the incarcerated women I met through them impacted me and refined my understanding of where my efforts were most needed. A poignant question from one of the women we represented stayed with me: "What about my kids?"

This question pierced me and redirected my focus toward the often-overlooked victims of the criminal legal system— the children. My career began to take a turn toward more direct activism.

During this time, the full weight of my mission became clear. The conversations with incarcerated women in Alabama and Louisiana, who continually voiced concerns over their children, had left a lasting imprint on me. Their stories of separation and longing shifted my focus from legal remedies to more holistic support. The decision to step away from practicing law wasn't taken lightly, but it felt like the only right move if I was to make a difference in justice-impacted women's lives and, by extension, their children's.

This shift in perspective culminated in many moments of self-reflection and internal struggle, challenging me to examine my true motivations and aspirations. I reflected on the legal profession's emphasis on status and material success, which were not the tenets the legal group I worked with endorsed, nor had they ever resonated with my deeper aspirations. It wasn't about gaining recognition for myself but making substantial changes in neglected or misunderstood areas. For me, that was about being in the perfect will of God.

Motivated by this spiritual awakening, the idea of starting a nonprofit began to form. This wasn't about a career shift but a call to fulfill a higher purpose. The vision was clear: to create an organization that went beyond traditional direct service by nurturing and supporting the self-determination and empowerment of children and their families, especially those from justice-impacted backgrounds, as they rose above their challenging circumstances.

The transition from law to nonprofit leadership was filled with challenges and excitement. It involved redefining what success meant to me—shifting from legal victories to making a tangible difference in the lives of people and the larger community. Our nonprofit aimed to be a beacon of hope, providing educational and personal growth opportunities and strengthening family bonds for those who needed them most – children with a parent in prison.

I directed my energies toward creating a space where the most vulnerable could find advocacy and support. This wasn't just about a handout, which is often what society thinks when we say nonprofit or charity, but about holistic support that addressed educational needs, emotional healing, and community empowerment. My nonprofit began to evolve into a sanctuary where children with a parent in prison could find safety and opportunity, families could seek assistance in rebuilding their lives, and the community, which had members who were justice-impacted, could learn to advocate for itself.

The work was challenging, no doubt, with each day presenting a new hurdle to overcome, from fundraising woes to bureaucratic tangles. Yet, each small victory brought immense satisfaction. The smiles of children learning in a safe environment, the gratitude of parents finding support in their darkest times, and the justice-impacted community growing stronger and more cohesive were my new measures of success.

Each step of building the organization, from writing our mission statement to engaging with community leaders, was a labor of love and conviction. Despite the hurdles—raising money for prisoners, an unpopular group in society, assembling the right team, navigating bureaucratic obstacles, and policies that were anti-family—the sense of purpose was overwhelming.

Reconnecting with my former sociology professor, Dr. Paula Dressel, when I returned to Atlanta post-law school marked another pivotal chapter in my journey. As fate would have it, she would soon play a significant role in the unfolding story of my nonprofit.

When I shared with her the evolving vision of my work, her response was immediate and affirmative: "If you decide you want to do it, I'm with you." Her involvement extended far beyond mere encouragement.

True to her word, she became the first president of our board. Together, we crafted the policies that would define our organization, including a socially responsible fundraising strategy that allowed us to maintain our integrity and independence from restrictive federal funding and foundation prescriptive largess but also a policy that challenged our organizational viability.

Thanks to my professor's advocacy, we were allowed to use one of the GSU Sociology Department's empty, unused offices for the summer of 1987, and we began laying the groundwork for what our agency would become. Weekly breakfast meetings with another close friend, Diana McDonald, at a local restaurant became the agency's brainstorming sessions, where ideas took shape over cups of coffee and shared aspirations.

One of my first initiatives was to visit women in Georgia prisons, not as their legal representative but as someone wanting to serve them in a new capacity. Their immediate and unanimous response—"Help me with my kids"—gave birth to one of our foundational programs, Family Visitation, facilitating visits between incarcerated mothers and their children. This program sought to maintain familial bonds and addressed both mothers and their children's emotional and psychological needs.

Staying true to the principle of listening to those we aimed to help rather than imposing our views became the cornerstone of our approach. It was crucial that those with lived experiences were not just heard but integral to our leadership. This ethos has guided our organization as it has grown and adapted.

The organization's growth was organic, fueled by the community's needs and the partnerships we formed. It wasn't the result of a large influx of capital or a singular monumental donation but rather the collective effort of many who shared our vision and mission. Therefore, the impact of our work cannot be measured in monetary terms alone but in the profound changes in the lives of those we've touched.

As I delve deeper into the layers of frontline practice, advocacy, and reform that have shaped my career, it's essential to understand our multi-faceted approach, from local initiatives to national movements. This journey isn't just about the work done in isolation in Atlanta but the interconnected efforts that span across states and ripple throughout the nation.

Starting in 1987, I was a fresh entrant into the realm of providing direct service and advocating for incarcerated women and their children. I sought to connect with others who shared this vision. My discoveries led me to pioneers like Ellen Barry in California and other formidable women across the country addressing similar issues. Ellen, a fellow lawyer, had established "Legal Services for Prisoners with Children."

A Massachusetts social worker, Jean Fox, had founded an organization dedicated to incarcerated mothers. Jean's innovative approach and focus on visits for the children with their mothers in MCI-Framingham, the oldest women's prison in the nation, provided inspiration and a framework upon which I could build.

Accompanied by my former sociology professor and the agency's inaugural board president, we attended a gathering in California, and joined forces with these incredible women to illuminate what was often an invisible issue. This collaboration strengthened the Roundtable on Women in Prison. In this national forum, we, with input from those with the lived experience of incarceration, could strategize and advocate for systemic change. It was a space that fostered dialogue and action, bringing the plight of incarcerated women and their children to the forefront of social justice conversations.

Statewide efforts in Georgia mirrored this national momentum. Working with the Department of Corrections in the late 80s, we established a Children's Center at the only women's prison in Hardwick, GA. That facility closed, but our work there was the model for the Children's Centers in all the women's prisons in Georgia.

Through a partnership in the early 2000s with the Department of Children and Family Services, under the leadership of Beverly Joe (BJ) Walker, who was the Commissioner of the Georgia Department of Human Resources and an Annie E. Casey fellow like me, we developed training curriculums for social workers, introducing protocols that recognized and addressed the specific needs of children with incarcerated parents. This was about more than awareness; it was about creating practical solutions that could be implemented across the state. Our initiatives led to establishing child-centered visitation in every transitional center in Georgia during Keith Horton's tenure as the GA Director of Child Services.

The partnerships that enhanced the bonds between incarcerated children and their parents testify to the agency's programmatic success and a model for other states to follow.

In Georgia, our commitment has been unwavering. Since 1987, our organization has never missed a scheduled visit to the prisons, coordinating trips for children to reunite with their incarcerated parents until 2020, when the global challenges posed by the pandemic, changed all aspects of life, including community-based organizations' access to correctional institutions.

When the prisons closed, it was a harsh setback, but our resolve didn't waver. Once they reopened, we worked with the GA Department of Corrections to regain access, and our efforts bore fruit in 2023 when we successfully organized trips for 1,500 children, facilitating precious reunions and supporting families who had not seen each other in three years.

The essence of our work lies in its grassroots nature— listening to and addressing the community's immediate needs while laying the groundwork for broader policy shifts. Every step forward is driven by the principle that those directly affected by the policies should have a voice in shaping them. This is not just about providing services; it's about empowering individuals to take control of their destinies and fostering an environment where they can thrive.

The philosophy of our organization reflects a deep-seated commitment to addressing the often unseen and unheard struggles of families torn apart by incarceration. This dedication is not merely operational but deeply personal, driven by the realities of children and parents who find themselves in the heartrending situation of separation due to the penal system.

Furthermore, the collateral damage of parental incarceration shows up in the statutory framework of the child welfare system. It often leads to severing parental rights if there has been no contact for a period, typically 15-out of 22 months[10]. This legislation, ostensibly designed to protect children, does not always consider the nuanced realities faced by those within the prison system. This policy realization was pivotal, compelling us to navigate these troubled waters with sensitivity and pragmatism.

Our agency decided early on to focus our resources where we could be most effective and cause the least harm. If a parent's rights were terminated, we generally stepped back to avoid giving false hope. Reestablishing parental rights under such circumstances is fraught with legal complexities and emotional turmoil. Instead, our efforts pivoted towards

---

[10] Child Welfare Information Gateway. (2021). Grounds for involuntary termination of parental rights. U.S. Department of Health and Human Services, Administration for Children and Families, Children's Bureau. https://www. childwelfare.gov/topics/systemwide/lawspolicies/statutes/groundtermin/

preventive measures and supporting ongoing parental relationships where legally feasible.

Addressing the needs of pregnant incarcerated women introduced another layer of complexity to our mission. The stark reality these women face—being shackled during childbirth and having only fleeting moments with their newborns before separation—is a harsh indictment of the system. Human Rights Watch's investigations into these practices underscored the urgent need for reform and fueled our commitment to these vulnerable members of our community. I applaud the work of Pamela Winn, founder of RestoreHer.US America (https://www.restoreher.us/), who has worked to ensure anti-shackling policies at the federal and state levels.

Our approach has always been to collaborate with like-minded organizations to form a cohesive front. Our collaboration with MotherhoodBeyond Bars (https://www.motherhoodbeyond.org/) extends our reach since they work directly with women in prison to ensure that the plan for the baby who must separate from their mom who returns to prison are in place. These partnerships are vital, enabling us to provide comprehensive support that includes not just visitation but also essential supplies and emotional support for pregnant women and their families.

This holistic method ensures that while we focus on facilitating child visitations, we also support broader services, advocacy, and reform efforts. This includes working on issues like shackling during childbirth, a practice we vehemently oppose, and promoting better conditions for pregnant inmates. Our combined efforts aim to create an environment where mothers can maintain a connection with their children, which is crucial for their mutual emotional well-being.

Through these collaborative efforts, we have advocated for and implemented significant changes within the system. Establishing children's centers in transitional facilities across Georgia is a testament to our commitment to fostering these vital maternal and parental bonds. These centers, primarily male facilities, are designed to facilitate meaningful interactions between parents and their children, ensuring the connection remains strong even when faced with constraints.

Additionally, our involvement doesn't end at the prison gates. Recognizing the financial burdens these visits can impose on families, we provide support such as meal vouchers and transportation assistance, ensuring that these reunions are accessible to all who need them. This aspect of our work is crucial, as it removes barriers to maintaining familial bonds, often strained by incarceration.

In every facet of our operations, including direct service, our focus remains steadfast—keeping the fundamental needs of the children, their caregivers, primarily women, and their incarcerated parents at the forefront of our mission. By maintaining this focus, we aid those directly affected and contribute to broader societal change, advocating for policies that recognize and address the complex realities of families impacted by parental incarceration.

Our understanding of these family dynamics—where children often stay with maternal relatives when a mother is incarcerated and a mix of paternal and maternal caregivers when it's the father—has shaped our approach. Recognizing the existing support systems that women naturally extend to each other, we tailored our efforts to enhance these networks rather than supplant them. For instance, instead of organizing new transportation to men's prisons, we supported the women already facilitating these visits, offering gas cards and covering lodging expenses for long trips, reinforcing their existing supportive structures.

Since 1987, our impact has reached over 45,000 children and their families, which signifies not just quantitative success, but a multitude of individual lives touched, transformed, and supported through their most challenging times. My commitment saw me participating in every prison visitation trip for the first two decades, driven by the belief that the children did not need people coming in and out of their lives like a revolving door. They needed people who were solidly entrenched in their lives and got to know them, their parents, and family members.

A key component of our approach was to support the family as they worked to maintain a semblance of normalcy for these children, which was crucial. It wasn't just about the frequency of visits but the quality and impact of those interactions. To further normalize their experiences, we initiated the first summer camp and counseling program in Georgia specifically for children of incarcerated parents, focusing on their unique psychological and emotional needs.

One of the most poignant moments in my journey was a bus ride with a young girl named Angel, which underscored the profound misunderstanding many of these children face about their circumstances. As we prepared to disembark the bus, I noticed her reluctance. Her innocent query, whether all the other children were visiting her mother too, revealed her isolation and confusion. This encounter vividly highlighted the importance of our work—not just in facilitating visits but in fostering a community among these children, letting them know they were not alone in their experiences.

The impact of our work has also been recognized and validated by the life trajectories of those we've supported. Numerous young people who have benefited from our programs have gone on to pursue higher education, often supported by scholarships we provide, join the military, start businesses, or enter trade schools. Our board has come to include adults who were once part of our programs as children, embodying the principle that those with lived experience should lead.

Our organizational ethos extends beyond the direct services we provide. We have consistently prioritized the dignity and privacy of the families we serve over potential media exposure or financial gain. Despite opportunities to gain national attention through platforms like Oprah's Angel

Network, created in the 90s to get people to use their lives to make a difference in the lives of others and interactions with other prominent media figures, we chose to protect the anonymity and integrity of our families.

These opportunities were not inherently bad, but the guiding philosophy of their interaction with people, which focused on telling your story, especially in sensational ways, was not the most sensitive to the children or empowering for the families on the outside. While costly in terms of potential funding and public recognition, our decision to stand with the families and honor what they want in terms of their privacy has been essential in maintaining the trust and respect of the communities we serve.

This book is more than a recounting of past deeds; it is a manifesto of our ongoing commitment and a call to action. It reflects on the sacrifices made in pursuing a mission that transcends individual gain, driven by a vision of what is just and good.

Through these pages, I aim to convey the challenges and successes we've encountered and the enduring values that have guided our work. This is how we know we've made a difference, and this is how we continue to move forward, committed to serving and uplifting those who need it most.

I realized that the extensive work I had been devoted to with the organization was only part of my larger calling. My experiences ingrained a deep understanding of the systemic issues facing marginalized communities, particularly girls, the fastest-growing population of incarcerated females in juvenile facilities, a topic that resonated deeply with me.

Our successful pilot program in Macon for teenage girls in the mid-2000s was a testament to our practical approach, ensuring these young women had the emotional support that they needed to rebuild their lives and in cases where they were mothers or had a mother in an adult facility, there was support and understanding of parental incarceration and what it requires.

My journey took a personal turn when I decided to retire from the organization I had founded and led. This was not a retreat from my mission but a strategic shift to ensure my own sustainability while continuing to contribute meaningfully to the sector. The decision was catalyzed during a meeting with a financial planner, who highlighted the precarious nature of my financial health after years of minimal compensation. His advice was stark yet necessary, urging me to consider the longevity of my ability to contribute and care for myself.

The transition to focusing fully on my consulting business, Sandra Barnhill and Associates, was both a personal and professional rebirth. I began to charge for the consulting services I previously offered for free, recognizing the value of my expertise and the necessity of building a sustainable business model. This shift was about more than just financial gain; it was about setting a precedent that valued my contributions while allowing me to maintain my commitment to social justice.

Creating a five-year plan for my business was a crucial part of this new phase. The plan wasn't just about business growth; it was about creating a stable foundation that would allow me to retire comfortably while continuing to support the causes dear to me. The pandemic delayed my planned retirement, but it also presented new opportunities for my business.

For the first time, I began thinking deeply about how I could work directly with and support the work of nonprofits and leaders who work at the frontlines tackling tough social justice issues or who bring their lived experiences to the work so that the theory of change becomes more nuanced. The shift to remote work also expanded my reach and allowed me to offer services, such as nonprofit consulting, to a wider audience, thus increasing the impact of my work.

I officially retired from the organization in 2024, recognizing that the world had changed irreversibly due to COVID-19. However, my commitment remained steadfast. I made a sacrificial pledge to help start the organization's endowment, a testament to my ongoing dedication to supporting the work I helped pioneer. This pledge was not just a financial contribution but a call to action for others in my network to support a cause that has given so much to the community. I am grateful for the core group of early donors to the endowment fund. In addition to being a regular donor over the next few years, my work is to create a campaign to grow the endowment significantly.

This new chapter isn't just about personal financial security; it's about leveraging my accumulated knowledge and experience to continue making a difference. My consulting work now includes advising senior nonprofit leaders, training and capacity building for nonprofits and social enterprises, and helping them navigate the complexities of funding, management, and sustainable impact. It continues my life's work, allowing me to support and empower the next generation of social sector leaders.

In the remaining chapters, I will share insights into how I stayed the course for almost forty years. I am often asked to mentor people, and I wish I could directly mentor more people than I do. However, I hope that the information I share will become a resource that activists can use to do social change work, whether they engage for a lifetime or a project, in a way that builds our community and enhances their personal quality of life.

Chapter 8: Debunking Myths About Activism

If we want to draw more people to activism, whether as a career or episodically, it's crucial to peel back the misconceptions surrounding activism, a realm often shrouded in romanticized narratives that do us more harm than good. We dwell in a society marred by racism, sexism, and other "isms'. As activists striving for change, we aren't immune to these influences. Acknowledging this reality is the first step in bringing our truest selves to the work that demands our best. It is also the first step in healing many wounds that we activists have received while doing this work and have also inflicted on other activists that we work with and potential activists as they make forays into our movement world.

In discussing the myths that surround our profession, it's essential to confront the harmful stereotypes that suggest activists are either superhuman or severely flawed. We are either romanticized or demonized. Such misconceptions misrepresent who we are and deter everyday people from joining our ranks, believing that activism is beyond their reach or requires a sacrifice of personal life and happiness. This couldn't be further from the truth. Activism isn't about losing our personal life but enriching it with purpose and passion.

One myth I want to dismantle right off the bat is the idea that *"activists don't have a life."*

Many assume that dedicating oneself to activism means abandoning hope for a balanced personal life. This misconception stems from tales of tireless fighters who never falter or fail—legends who live only for the cause. While the dedication of such individuals is admirable, it paints a picture that's unrealistic and unattainable for most.

The truth is that activists are just like everyone else. We juggle personal responsibilities, experience burnout, and indeed, we have days when we don't feel like championing the cause. We struggle with the pressure to be politically correct, to check all the boxes, and to ensure that our actions and words do not exclude or marginalize. This ongoing effort to balance our ideals with the practical demands of activism can be overwhelming.

I confess there are days when I need to get things done without the extensive conversations, all the processing and collaborations that are typically required. In these moments, I might revert to traditional roles or take on more than my share to push through the tasks at hand. However, I always strive to return to my foundational commitment to inclusivity and shared responsibility once the immediate pressure eases. This cycle reminds me that we are all a work in progress.

The key takeaway is that being an activist involves constant self-reflection and mastery. It's about recognizing when we fall short and not being too hard on ourselves when we do. It's also about not getting overly self-congratulatory when we succeed. Maintaining this balanced view helps us stay grounded and focused on the long-term goals rather than getting caught up in momentary wins or losses.

This book aims to start a conversation about these issues—to challenge both seasoned and new activists to think critically about what it means to be an activist. It's for anyone who has ever felt discouraged by stereotypes or judged by the unrealistic standards often imposed on us.

By deconstructing these myths, we can begin to foster a more inclusive and realistic understanding of activism—one that allows for personal growth, embraces our imperfections and acknowledges that each of us, regardless of how experienced or devoted, is navigating our unique journey towards creating change. In doing so, we invite more people to join us, reassured that they don't have to be perfect to make a difference. After all, activism is a collective endeavor, not a heroic solo venture.

Let's dismantle a particularly tenacious myth that has long shrouded the world of activism:

Myth No. 1: Good Activists Are Martyrs

In the gritty narrative of social movements, there's a storied tradition of valorizing those who sacrifice it all for the cause. This notion of martyrdom—of giving up everything from personal health to family ties for the movement—has often been held up as the gold standard for what it means to be a "real" activist. We've all heard the tales, told with a mix of weariness and pride: endless nights preparing for a rally, cobbling together protest signs, the sleep-deprived vigilance during threats to our community centers, or the mad dashes to assist a comrade in crisis, foregoing sleep and sanity. These stories, recounted with gusto, have become our war medals, worn ostentatiously and with pride.

Historically, this glorification of self-sacrifice has been gendered in its recognition. Men's martyr-like stamina in activism is often celebrated unambiguously. However, when a woman dedicates herself similarly, societal perceptions become double-edged. Suppose she's without a partner or children. In that case, her devotion is sometimes lauded, albeit patronizingly framed as her having replaced personal relationships with the cause—implying that her commitment is compensatory for a lack in her personal life. If she is a mother or a wife, her commitment is scrutinized and often unfairly critiqued behind closed doors.

The consequences of this martyrdom myth are far from heroic; they are profoundly damaging. I've seen too many brilliant minds succumb to the darker corners of depression, turn to substances as coping mechanisms, or lash out in frustration—even against those on their team. Worse yet, some completely burn out and step away from the activism that once fueled their fire. Now, it's clear to me that framing such self-destructive tendencies as prerequisites for genuine activism does a disservice to us all. It creates an unsustainable model where the people striving for change are broken by the process, often before they can see the fruits of their labor.

We're in this movement not just to exist but to thrive and effect real, tangible change. We need everyone well in body, spirit, mind, and health. Encouraging or even tacitly endorsing the depletion of our ranks through unchecked martyrdom undercuts our goals. We cannot afford to romanticize or perpetuate the narrative that to be a real activist, one must forsake all else. This is neither practical nor healthy, and it certainly isn't sustainable.

Instead, I advocate for a new paradigm in activism, one where self-care is as integral as strategic planning and organizing in the streets. To paraphrase author and equal rights activist Audre Lorde, caring for oneself is not selfish but self-preservation. She is right. It is how we ensure we're fighting fit for the long haul. I want us to redefine what strength looks like in our circles. It's not about how much we can endure before breaking—it's about fostering resilience, creating supportive networks, and empowering each individual to contribute in a personally healthy and sustainable manner.

We must dismantle the dangerous myth that activists must live in perpetual sacrifice. I don't want heroes martyred by their own dedication; I want comrades alive and vibrant, actively participating in the joyous celebration of our collective achievements. Our stories shouldn't just be about survival through adversity but about thriving amidst the challenge, fostering a movement that nurtures as much as it agitates.

As we move forward, let's commit to protecting our ranks from burnout, celebrating balanced lives, and ensuring that our activism is a testament to the world we're fighting to create—one where equity, respect, and health are foundational values. Let's live for our cause with such vitality and joy that we inspire change in society and a transformation in how activism is perceived and practiced.

Myth No. 2: Good Activists are Broke

Tackling another pervasive myth in the activism community that often goes unspoken yet looms large and controversial: the notion that true activists must embrace poverty. According to this myth, authenticity in activism is measured by a lack of material wealth. If I drive a nice car, live in a well-appointed home, or—God forbid—reside outside an inner-city area, whispers start circulating that I might just be a traitor to the cause.

This myth has flared into the spotlight recently, with notable figures in movements like Black Lives Matter facing backlash for their personal success. The criticism often hinges on a perceived betrayal of activist values, as if financial stability somehow dilutes one's commitment to social change. This notion taps into deeper, troubling undercurrents of cancel culture, where the court of public opinion is quick to label and even quicker to condemn without understanding the broader context.

Let's unpack this: everyone has the right to determine their own needs, including what they need to feel safe, rested, and find peace. For some, that might mean living in a gated community. I'm not here to judge that choice. What matters is not where we lay our heads at night but where we stand when it counts. Those gates might indeed come down one day, and when they do, we'll need to know whether we stand with the gatekeepers or the people tearing them down.

Being financially stable or even wealthy doesn't automatically sever your ties to the movement or diminish your role within it. The key is to stay connected and maintain genuine, active links to the community you live in and serve. It's entirely possible to live comfortably and still be deeply committed to driving change.

However, there's a delicate balance to strike. Wealth can create barriers, both visible and invisible. If we're not careful, it can isolate us from the very people we're advocating for. The challenge lies in ensuring that our financial success doesn't insulate us from the realities those less fortunate face. It's about leveraging our resources to further the cause, not shielding ourselves from the struggle's harsher truths.

Moreover, we must confront the stigmatization within our ranks that equates financial hardship with activist purity. It may stem from the very low wages frontline activists make, but regardless, this stigma is damaging—it perpetuates a narrative that to be a "real" activist, we must sacrifice our time, energy, and our chance at a stable, secure life. It's a narrative that burns people out and drives them away, exactly the opposite of what our movements need.

We should promote sustainability in activism. It's about making activism a viable long-term commitment if you choose to do so, without having to endure periods of financial martyrdom, which, even if short, take a toll on our financial future. We need activists who can stay in the fight for the long haul and aren't preoccupied with financial survival to the extent that it hampers their ability to effect change.

In short, breaking down this myth isn't just about allowing activists to enjoy a higher standard of living; it's about enriching the movement with their prolonged, effective participation. True activism isn't about how much you suffer financially but how effectively you can fight for the cause. Sometimes, having resources can make us more effective fighters.

So, if living in comfort, driving a reliable car, or even enjoying some luxury helps us stay energized and committed, then it's not just a personal benefit—it's a boon for the movement. Let's redefine what it means to be a "good" activist: not by the scarcity of our possessions but by the abundance of our contributions to the cause.

Myth No. 3: Activists Need to Fight 24/7

One of the most exhausting myths I've encountered throughout my activism journey is the notion that to be a truly committed activist, we must always be in battle mode. This idea can drain even the most passionate among us. In reality, embracing moments of peace and nurturing personal joy is crucial for longevity in activism and essential for maintaining mental and emotional health.

Later in this book, I discuss the importance of finding inner peace and carving out a personal vision that resonates with who we are. For me, that vision is deeply tied to peace and harmony. Over the years, taking various personality tests like Myers-Briggs has consistently shown that I thrive in harmonious environments. This understanding has shaped how I construct my inner circle and personal spaces.

In my life, I've made a conscious decision to surround myself with tranquility. This means I deliberately choose not to include individuals in my inner circle who thrive on chaos or those who constantly challenge my peace. It's not that I shy away from debate or differing opinions—these are essential in our lives and our work. However, my home and closest relationships must be sanctuaries of support and respect, not extensions of the battlegrounds I face in my activism.

Having peace at home doesn't mean I'm less committed to the causes I fight for. Rather, it ensures that I'm recharged and resilient when I step into the fray. Like anyone else, I need a respite from the constant high energy of activism. At home, I create an environment filled with things that soothe me—soft music, the gentle glow of candlelight, the calming sound of water from my pond, and the lushness of green plants. These aren't just decorative choices; they're necessities that help me maintain my well-being.

Part of our 24/7 world is work, so increasingly, I am examining how I engage in social change work when working with other activists. Yes, we will have disagreements and passionately see things differently, but do we have to destroy each other in the process?

I believe the adage hurt people, hurt people. Hence, as I do the work, I want to be committed to doing my personal work and dealing with and healing from my issues and trauma. I also want to make sure that I am working with activists who are willing to do their interior work so that our actions and words reflect people on a healing journey, which means we don't bring a " scorched earth" mentality to work which often manifests in destructive activities such as competing, judging, tearing each other down, spewing bitterness or having constant drama when peace could prevail if given a chance.

Let's debunk the idea that to be a 'real' activist, you must live in a perpetual state of conflict or aggression. This myth is harmful and can lead to burnout and disillusionment. Instead, I advocate for a balanced approach where activists take intentional breaks and engage in activities that replenish their spirits and give them opportunities for rest and peace.

These activities are vital. Whether it's tucking the kids into bed a bit early so you can chill, retreating to a quiet space to recharge before re-engaging with family or friends, cooking for pleasure rather than necessity, taking a daily walk, practicing yoga, scheduling a mental health day or days off from work, fasting from the news or taking a vacation which does not mean you have to travel far or spend a lot of money, you can have a staycation. They are not distractions from our mission but essential practices that sustain our ability to continue the movement.

Moreover, embracing love and allowing yourself to experience deep, meaningful relationships are crucial. Love, in its healthiest form, should feed your soul and elevate your spirit. It's the most potent force in the universe, and to deny yourself this experience is to miss out on a fundamental aspect of life.

Remember, taking care of yourself isn't a betrayal of your activism; it's an integral part of it. By ensuring you are physically, mentally, and emotionally fit, you are better equipped to meet the demands of activism head-on. This balance between action and rejuvenation keeps you effective over the long haul, ensuring you survive the battles and thrive in life overall.

So, let's shift the narrative. Let's model a form of activism that values well-being as much as fervor, that sees the activist not as a martyr but as a whole human being capable of leading a balanced, fulfilling life while making impactful changes. This isn't just about sustaining the movement; it's about thriving within it, ensuring we all have the longevity to see the fruits of our labor and the joy of our efforts.

Myth No. 4: Activists Aren't Racist or Sexist

We live in a society steeped in racism and sexism, and the uncomfortable truth is that those of us striving for change are not immune to these afflictions. The belief that activists are somehow exempt from racist or sexist attitudes is a myth that undermines the integrity of our work. It's crucial to acknowledge that racism and sexism can and do permeate the activist community, and failing to confront this reality means we are not bringing our best selves to the cause.

The prevalence of racism and sexism within activist circles is a painful irony, given that so many social movements owe their momentum—and often their very existence—to Black people and women, particularly Women of Color. Despite this, there remains a persistent tendency to sideline their contributions, to diminish their roles to the peripheries of the narrative, even when they are at the heart of these movements.

I want to say upfront that one "ism" isn't more important than the other. We need to address racism, sexism, and all the other isms. I am a Black woman, and I have experienced many of the "isms," so I call for the eradication of all of them!

While racism is very much alive in the nonprofit world, I want to talk specifically about sexism here because in the independent sector (and in the profit-making world), women generally receive the lowest wages on the pay scale and perform much of the low-wage labor, whether it be through thought leadership, direct service, or advocacy.

Historical and ongoing movements worldwide underscore this point. Women have participated in, led, and sustained many of these struggles. From the resistance against the Trujillo dictatorship in the Dominican Republic to the women's peer groups in India fighting against child marriage, women have been at the forefront.

In the United States, women have held and continue to hold leadership roles in the Civil Rights Movement, the Peace Movement, and the Black Lives Matter Movement. Yet, despite such significant contributions, the acknowledgment and recognition of women as strategists, collaborators, revolutionaries, warriors, and leaders have been scant.

This book aims to shift that narrative by intentionally elevating my voice and the voices of women activists. Recognizing our contributions and our unique challenges within these spaces is essential. Women are often dubbed "mothers of the movement," a title that reflects our nurturing roles but also hints at the gendered expectations placed upon us. These roles extend beyond organizing and strategizing; they include feeding, cleaning, and caring for the community—vital but often undervalued tasks.

The superwoman role attributed to women in activism carries a double-edged sword. There is a certain respect and honor associated with being able to manage multiple responsibilities efficiently. However, this often comes with a patriarchal twist where women are expected to uphold and perpetuate these roles without complaint. When women fail to meet these superhuman expectations, the repercussions are severe: we are often omitted from history books, excluded from crucial meetings, or asked to step aside to make room for male leaders.

The consequences for women who challenge these sexist norms can be severe. We face professional setbacks, such as being overlooked for leadership roles or excluded from key strategic discussions and subject to personal attacks that question our commitment and integrity as activists. This perpetuates a cycle where women are simultaneously needed for the success of movements but not allowed to thrive within them fully.

Addressing sexism in activism isn't just about fairness or equity; it's necessary to advance any social justice agenda effectively. Recognizing the contributions of women, dismantling the structures that marginalize us, and valuing our work appropriately are fundamental to the health and success of any movement. As we move forward, we must challenge these outdated narratives and work towards a genuinely inclusive activism environment where everyone's contribution is acknowledged and valued. This is not just a fight for the rights of those we advocate for but also a fight within our ranks to ensure we embody our principles.

Below, I share some personal examples of how sexism has manifested in the activist community over the last three decades. As you read the scenarios, you will see that as society has evolved and certain behaviors have become unacceptable, the displays of sexism have also changed.

Being asked to take notes in a meeting—When asked, I'd say, "No. Why don't you take notes or ask one of the men here to take notes?"

I am a bit of a disruptor, so that was always funny to me because it would temporarily shut the meeting down. The men would look down at the paper or the nonexistent form in their hand, never at their notepad, laptop, tablet, or phone – all devices for notetaking or looking around, not at the men, but for another woman to step up and save them. And often, some good daughter of the patriarchy would raise her hand or say, "Okay, I'll just take the notes."

And she'd do it in a way that allowed her to express some level of disgust in solidarity with me, but she would still feel the need to "just do it."

I understood that.

Regardless of our calling or life's work, most of us are hesitant or even refuse to challenge the authority we respect. Something about freedom, justice, and liberation movements makes us take a step back before challenging intergroup authority.

It could be rooted in the fact that we understand the importance of our work and how so few are willing to do it. So, we come to the table recognizing that most of us there have already counted the cost we'll pay to do the work, and we're willing to pay it. We don't want to add to that cost, so we try hard to make things work. We know our authority as a group of people is frequently undermined, so we try to compensate for some of that by giving our leaders a wide berth and not challenging them unless we feel it's absolutely necessary.

I approach my comrades differently as I've gotten older and more experienced. When no staff is assigned to handle notetaking, I often talk more about our collective memorialization of the meeting and how each of us can take a piece of that work.

Picking up the refreshments— Women are primarily asked to pick up the refreshments or order food on the app. Hospitality does not have "women only" on the label or "women first." I wasn't born knowing how to figure out the quantities to feed large crowds or the right amount of food to order; I had to figure it out and learn by doing. I am a vegetarian, and after I order the food a time or two and my food choices are too healthy, they don't ask me to figure out the order; they do that and want me to place it.

Putting or pulling it all together— If you are a woman, you are still asked to pull things together, often at the last moment. While they might express appreciation to you and build your reputation in the movement as a sister who will get things done, they often don't consider the personal cost for you.

So, what I've learned to do now is to set some ground rules and make it clear before we start doing the work that it's collective work and responsibility. We can all take turns, pair up, and do whatever we want, but it needs to be clear that it's not always going to be my turn. And a lot of times, I raise that in that way so as not to challenge good brothers and good daughters of the patriarchy.

Malcolm X said, *"By any means necessary."*

There are so many different stereotypes of women who do movement work. I am a single woman, and one of the stereotypes, particularly about single women who do movement work, is that we don't have anything else to do anyway.

"Sister such and such or brother such and such, has children or has a family, so if you can stay late and do the extra stuff…" If you dare say, "No, I can't. I've got something planned," they look at you like, "What? You don't have a family," not realizing that you are your family and you have folks who love you, care for you, nurture you, and help you feel connected that you need to be with, too.

And that's just as important as "biological family," which proves that none of us are immune to very traditional, sexist views.

So, I say thank you to myself and every single sister in the movement who has stayed late so that someone else can go home to the kids or the spouse. Thank you! Our sacrifice and our work have made a difference. At the same time, I want to encourage us to just say no. That three-letter word, yes, gets way too much play in the world at large and in activist work specifically.

Just say no.

Better yet, say no and don't explain. It's not, "No, because I gotta go to blah, blah, blah." It's no because I'm saying no. And whatever the reason, whether it stems from wanting to go home and read a good book, take a bubble bath, hang out with friends, or I don't feel like it, or because I've got something else I want to do. Whatever the reason, no is okay and is what we must model and teach through our actions, not just our words.

Sexism didn't leave, miss, or avoid the social justice movements. Our work must be to change that. But it can't just be women's work. We also need men and boys to practice liberatory principles, beliefs, and actions toward women. Our work must be done in spaces where men and women are present, and especially in private spaces where there are only men.

Words, thoughts, actions, and deeds that don't uplift and support women must be denounced, especially in all-male settings. The men who are present must address the behavior of men who discount and disrespect women and think it is okay because they are in men's spaces and no women are around to hear it. In all spaces, women must be recognized as leaders, collaborators, conspirators, and workers who take care of children, cook, and clean with men, not for men.

Subset of the Activists Aren't Racist, or Sexist is the Myth that Black Women Are Superwomen

Finally, I want to address a specific challenge that I struggle to address in my own practice and have observed in others' practices: we praise and vilify strength, especially the strength of Black women who have endured so much and are still standing. Yes, we are beautiful, strong, and powerful, but the world often fails to allow us to be strong enough to be gentle.

Throughout much of my career, I struggled with this paradox. There was a time when I couldn't cry; I'd been through so much; things had deeply wounded me, and I felt numb. Even when barely standing, I was still expected to carry others. This expectation wasn't just from others but also myself—I allowed it.

When I finally focused on my needs, whether to experience joy, engage in an interesting activity, or take a break, I was often met with remarks like, "What? You can't get tired."

To myself and my beautiful Black sisters, I say: do not let the world, whether the larger world or the activist community, define us. If we are in a space that doesn't allow us to rest, enjoy life, or find balance, leave that space!

If the people around us refuse to let us off the treadmill, fail to recognize that we can't carry everyone, or deny us what we critically need, we must distance ourselves from them. If they don't support our well-being now, they never will. We must create a better reality, starting with admitting when we are tired, overwhelmed, and have had enough.

Admitting we sometimes need a break is frightening yet essential. For me, it took the exhaustion of 20 years of work to learn how to prioritize rest and acknowledge that rest was not just what I finally got when I got some sleep or when the crisis was over. That doesn't work because the crisis may not be yours, but others seem to be in play 24/7. Rest is an activity I need to engage in daily. Trica Hershey, the founder of the Nap Ministry and the author of *Rest is Resistance*, says rest is our birthright.

Sometimes, when I talk about resting, the response I get is, "I will rest when I die." I reject that response. It is not valid to me. I want us to rest so we live and don't die!

I've also accepted that some people never want me to take a break. That's their vision for me, their expectation, and I cannot always fulfill it—nor should I. What I must do is be true to myself. The clarion call must come from me. I need to ask and answer for myself: What do I critically need?

The phrase "What do I critically need?" was coined by a Black woman, Anana Harris Parris, the founder of the Sister CARE Alliance and the Evolve Network. She wrote a book called *Self Care Matters: A Revolutionary Approach*, which expands on what I am discussing and offers practical self-care tools and tips.

One concept she discusses that resonates deeply with me is taking baby steps in self-care, making small, manageable changes that don't feel overwhelming or radical but can significantly impact your well-being. I encourage you to read her book.

A final word about the superwoman myth: Sisters, we must pull the cape off and kick it to the curb! We cannot let anyone pick it up and give it back to us or buy us a new one. We need to give our superwoman persona a big hug and tell her we love her, but she can't be on duty 24/7. While there are times when we need to don our capes and move forward as superwomen, we cannot sustain that role continuously.

When people comment on how super strong I am, suggesting I can do anything and handle everything even when I am exhausted, I am learning that it's okay to say, "Thanks, I appreciate the compliment. I'm just a woman who cares and wants to do her part. I am not a superwoman. I need rest and a break." Or, "Thank you for noticing I'm acting like a superwoman. That's not how I always want to show up, so I'm glad you recognized it and shared it with me because I am working on how I show up."

We're not trying to obliterate the superwoman; we're simply trying to give her some space, move her to the side, and put her in a resting position to be pulled out when absolutely necessary so that other, more realistic and less self-sacrificing images of us as Black women can emerge.

Myth No. 5: Activists Don't Engage in Colorism

It's the 21st century, but I feel the need to address this. Like racism and sexism, colorism is alive and well in the activist community, often shaping who gets media coverage, and who receives funding from foundations, corporations, and even individuals. It is a form of white supremacy.

As a Person of Color, I have to be very careful not to buy into colorism in my work and approach to movements. As most of us know, the way colorism works is that the lighter the person is, the closer their proximity to whiteness and the higher position society affords them. The closer you are to whiteness, the better you're perceived to be. My maternal grandmother, Lucille Bussey Monon, who was born in and never left the South, called it being "color-struck."

If proximity to whiteness gives privileges, then the darker you are, the more quickly and easily you are discounted. Many people think colorism occurs only among people of African descent. On the contrary, I've traveled all over the world and have seen consistently that the darker you are, whether you're Iranian, Brazilian, South Asian, Indian, or other nationality, the more your options are viewed as limited.

Proximity to whiteness is recognized globally. In his book *The Hidden Brain: How Our Unconscious Minds Elect Presidents, Control Markets, Wage Wars and Save Our Lives*, author Shankar Vedantam says, *"Colorism yields real-world advantages for individuals with light skin. For example, light-skinned Latinos make $5,000 more on average than dark-skinned Latinos."*

In the United States, colorism evolved when the enslavement of people was common practice. Enslavers typically gave preferential treatment to enslaved people with fairer complexions. While dark-skinned enslaved people toiled outdoors in the fields, their light-skinned counterparts usually worked indoors performing domestic tasks.

Enslavers were partial (if you can call any subhuman treatment partial) to light-skinned enslaved people because they often were family members. Enslavers frequently forced enslaved women into sex, and the light-skinned children of enslaved people were the telltale signs of these sexual assaults. While enslavers didn't officially recognize their mixed-race children, they gave them privileges that dark-skinned enslaved people didn't enjoy. Accordingly, light skin came to be viewed as an asset in the community of enslaved people.

Outside the United States, colorism may be more related to class than to white supremacy.[11]

I am a Black person who is not "light-skinned." I have experienced colorism from other Black people and People of Color. Their actions toward me are based on the darkness of my skin, perpetuating colorism and internalized oppression. Often, when I am leading, they look around at others who are present, whether facilitating or training with me at that moment, and immediately think they are the ones in charge, even if they are very young and obviously look like interns.

I have been in countless meetings, and when I say something, it is not acknowledged, but if a person who has closer proximity to whiteness says it, the idea becomes valuable and embraced. The fact that I raised it first is never

---

[11] Nittle, N. K. (2021, February 28). The roots of colorism, or skin tone discrimination. ThoughtCo. https://www.thoughtco.com/what-is-colorism-2834952

acknowledged. My decisions are often second-guessed, constantly challenged, or unfollowed because the person who gave the directive, me, is a darker-skinned person, and they are unsure what should be done since they are not used to taking direction from someone who looks like me.

When I have People of Color who have made unnecessary challenges to my authority in a situation, I wonder if colorism is at work. If they are open enough to dialogue about what is going on, I will ask if working with me is the first time they have taken leadership from a non-white person or a dark-skinned Black person. If that is too direct, I also ask them to reflect on how they have shown up in our interactions.

Did they challenge me constantly or have a hard time accepting my authority?

As a darker-skinned Black woman, I have often had not just white people but People of Color pull out the tools of white supremacy, the same ones that have been used against them, and use them on me. Colorism requires us to evaluate ourselves and our behavior and be honest about it.

As darker-skinned People of Color, we mustn't internalize our oppression to the point where because we are darker, we feel our ideas aren't as important that we need to be in the background, serving and never being served, or that we are more valuable if we're connected to a fairer-skinned person. Daily microagressions can make you feel that way. I have been in countless meetings, and when I say something, it is not acknowledged, but if a person who has closer proximity to whiteness says it, the idea becomes valuable.

In her book, *Tomorrow's Tomorrow,* the sociologist Dr. Joyce Ladner focuses on a study of black girls growing up in the Pruitt-Igoe housing projects in St. Louis, interviewing over 100 Black girls and emphasizing that we cannot allow others to define us. We must define ourselves. As Dr. Ladner states, *"Our self-definition is a radical act of reclaiming our humanity."*

Defining ourselves starts with rejecting rampant white supremacy. We must reject the thought processes it engenders and the actions that it perpetuates. All People of Color have been touched by this monster called racism and have had the tools of white supremacy used against us. I would venture to say that whether we want to admit it or not, we have also learned how to use those tools.

This is why I return to the very premise of this book: If you want to be an activist, an organizer, or a revolutionary, you must have a tough mind and a tender heart. A tough mind comes from examining yourself and your actions to develop a tender heart and empathy for people. A tough mind uses its intellect in service to the people, and a tender heart recognizes all of humanity, yours and that of others.

So, to People of Color, every shade in the rainbow, we are beautiful. We are powerful. We are at our best when we figure out how to work together. There is power in our numbers and purpose in all of our struggles. And while we don't do it nearly enough, we must have more cross-cultural dialogue. We must talk about what matters with one another and find the space and strength to hold one another accountable when we're doing and saying things that are less than liberating, healing, and affirming of ourselves, our brothers and sisters in the movement, and the people that we are fighting for.

Chapter 9: Knowing Yourself So You Can Speak Your Truth

In this chapter, I refer to "centered activism." I am unsure if it is a widely used term, but I have started using it because it speaks to the notion that being well-balanced in our movement work is important. To be well-balanced, we must know ourselves—the good, the bad, and the ugly—as we engage in activism, which is life-changing work for us as individuals, for the people we serve, and for the larger community.

Centered activism is not only about external actions it's equally about internal growth and alignment. Understanding oneself is foundational - a prerequisite to genuine and effective engagement with the world.

At the heart of centered activism lies the imperative to know yourself deeply. This introspection involves more than a superficial acknowledgment of one's likes and dislikes. It's about diving deep into one's values, beliefs, strengths, and vulnerabilities. It's about understanding your motivations, fears, and biases you carry. This self-awareness is crucial because it influences how you interact with the world, connect with others, and how resilient you are in the face of challenges.

Michelle Obama once said, *"One of the lessons that I grew up with was to always stay true to yourself and never let what somebody else says distract you from your goals."*

This advice encapsulates the essence of centered activism. Staying true to oneself isn't just about adherence to one's goals but also about the clarity and authenticity you bring to every action and decision. When you are grounded in a thorough understanding of yourself, you are less likely to be swayed by external pressures or distracted by superficial accolades. Your activism becomes a reflection of your deepest truths.

In the remaining pages of this chapter, I unpack many aspects of centered activism and offer them to you, the reader, as tools you can use as an activist, whether for the long haul or a short term or project basis, to get clarity on how to navigate with integrity and clarity in this contradictory world we live in. Specifically, I list check-in points, which are places of inquiry for you about your own practice and how you show up. I call them steps.

Step 1: Knowing Yourself

The journey of an activist begins with a simple yet profound question:

Do you know yourself—your true self?

How can you be sure of your self-knowledge?

This isn't about mere self-reflection or introspection for its own sake; it's about understanding that activism is often a direct extension of one's life purpose—a calling that transcends the conventional definition of a job.

For many, particularly those for whom this book is written, activism is not a trend or a social statement to garner "likes" on social media. It is not about being seen at the forefront of a movement to showcase one's wokeness. Instead, for activists, it represents a profound commitment to changing the world, an endeavor that defines their life's work which does not mean that they must accomplish everything in a sound bite.

Knowing yourself is imperative because it shapes how you engage with your cause. It determines your motivations, guides your actions, and helps you communicate your beliefs more effectively. It also aids in aligning your actions with your values, ensuring that your activism is not just an external show but a genuine expression of your deepest convictions.

But how do you know if you truly know yourself?

It begins with examining your motivations.

Are you driven by a desire for personal recognition, or are you genuinely committed to the cause?

Do your actions reflect a deep-seated belief in the change you advocate for, or are they influenced by external validation and the approval of peers?

For those deeply committed, activism is an integral part of their identity. It is not chosen lightly nor abandoned easily. It is chosen because it resonates deeply with their personal beliefs and values. This profound connection to their cause means that their activism is not merely something they do; it is a part of who they are.

This integration of personal identity with activist work necessitates a deep level of self-awareness. Without it, there's a risk of becoming disconnected from the cause, leading to burnout or disillusionment. Activists must continuously engage in self-reflection to ensure their work remains aligned with their core values and to prevent their mission from being swayed by the fleeting trends of activism that can dominate social media and public discourse.

Truly knowing yourself also means recognizing and embracing your unique strengths and acknowledging your weaknesses. It involves understanding your emotional triggers and learning how to manage them effectively. This self-awareness is crucial in navigating the often-tumultuous waters of social change, where conflicts and challenges are routine.

By grounding your activism in a solid understanding of your own identity, you build a resilient foundation that can withstand external pressures and internal doubts. This isn't just about steadfastness; it's about cultivating a form of activism that is sustainable, effective, and authentically connected to who you are.

The intriguing dynamic between the true self and the presented self is a distinction that's particularly relevant in today's culture, where the pressure to perform is pervasive. Understanding this dichotomy is crucial for activists, as it deeply influences personal identity and how effectively one can advocate for change without losing authenticity.

The concept of the *"true self"* refers to who we are at our core—our deepest values, unfiltered thoughts, emotions, and beliefs. It's the version of us that exists when there are no external pressures to conform or perform. In contrast, the *"presented self"* is the persona we project to the world, often shaped by societal expectations and the desire to be accepted or liked. This persona can sometimes be a far cry from who we genuinely are, tailored to fit into the various roles we play in society—be it as a professional, a friend, or even a family member.

In America, there's a significant emphasis on living up to the expectations of others. Our parents, mentors, friends, and even our social media followers can profoundly impact how we present ourselves. The danger here is that we can lose touch with our true selves by constantly striving to meet these external standards. The essence of who we are gets buried under layers of performed identities that may garner approval but leave us feeling hollow or unfulfilled.

We live in an era dominated by performance. The rise of reality TV, social media platforms like TikTok, and the ubiquitous use of Zoom have all heightened the sense of being perpetually 'on stage.' Performative culture demands that we are always ready to present an optimized version of ourselves that is palatable and appealing to a broad audience.

Consider this reflection by a cultural critic: *"In a world where reality feels increasingly like a spectacle, our true selves often become spectators to the personas we parade across the digital stage."*

This statement captures the essence of modern performative culture, where the lines between authenticity and performance blur, making it harder to distinguish genuine actions from those done for show.

Living authentically requires constant vigilance and courage, especially when societal norms demand conformity. It involves making deliberate choices to align your actions with your true self and resisting the allure of approval that comes with performing to others' expectations. This doesn't mean completely disregarding how others perceive you but rather not letting these perceptions dictate your self-worth or actions.

As activists, the integrity of our work depends significantly on our authenticity. If we preach social change but live inauthentically, we undermine our credibility and the effectiveness of our advocacy. Thus, reconnecting with our true selves is not just a personal journey; it's a professional imperative. It ensures that our passion for our causes is genuine and that our advocacy is rooted in deeply held beliefs rather than superficial commitments inspired by current trends or external validation.

In summary, understanding and embracing your true self in a culture dominated by performance is challenging but essential. It's about finding the strength to present your genuine self to the world, thereby fostering a deeper connection with your activism and living a life that truly reflects your values and ideals.

So, how can one reconnect with and define one's true self amid these pressures?

A foundational step is to identify and commit to your core values. These values are typically derived from various influences in your life—your upbringing, cultural background, religious beliefs, education, and personal heroes. They are the principles you want to govern your behaviors and decisions, regardless of external approval.

Step 2: Identifying and Choosing Core Values

To start, reflect on moments when you felt most fulfilled or at peace—chances are, these moments occurred when you were aligned with your core values. Write these down and consider how they manifest in your daily life and activism.

Are you living in harmony with these values, or are you often compelled to compromise them to fit a certain image or expectation?

Understanding the values that guide your behavior and decision-making is essential for personal alignment and effectively linking your values to your social justice work.

If the exercise above did not get you closer to knowing what your core values are or if you are still uncertain, here's a straightforward activity to help clarify them, inspired by insights from an article in Psychology Today titled *"6 Ways to Discover and Choose Your Core Values."*

1. Brainstorm Potential Values: If you did write down words during the previous exercise, use them or begin by writing down a list of characteristics that might represent your values. If you're unsure where to start, relax, take your time, and let the ideas flow naturally. It's best to do this with a pen or pencil—there's scientific evidence suggesting that the physical act of writing creates a stronger connection between thought and action, effectively embedding these concepts more deeply into your consciousness.

2. Admiration Reflection: Write a list of characteristics you admire in others. Aim for at least ten, and then prioritize this list to your top six. This exercise helps you identify qualities that resonate with you personally and are likely aligned with your own core values.

3. Role Model Values: Think of three to five people who you view as role models and list the values you believe they embody. This can provide insights into the values you aspire to integrate into your own life.

4. Self-Definition: List the top ten characteristics that define you. This step moves beyond admiration to personal identification, helping you see which values truly speak to your identity. Avoid editing or judging what comes to mind; some find it helpful to close their eyes and ask, "Who am I?" and then write down whatever comes to mind.

5. Link Values to Actions: Reflect on how these values could translate into social justice efforts. What issues or organizations resonate with these values? Identifying this connection can guide you toward activism that feels meaningful and is sustainable and impactful.

Step 3: Living and Acting from Your Core Values

Understanding your core values is foundational to effective activism. They shape how you engage with the world and dictate the causes you champion. For instance, if one of your core values is integrity, you might naturally oppose any form of injustice or dishonesty. This might manifest as calling out inappropriate behavior when others choose to stay silent.

For example, my commitment to integrity means I do not laugh along at sexist or racist jokes. Instead, I call out the person making the joke because my values compel me to challenge the status quo and hold others accountable, even when it's uncomfortable. This approach often makes people uneasy because it disrupts the norm and demands a higher standard of interaction.

Once you're clear on your core values, they become a compass guiding your actions and decisions in activism. These values help you select causes that align with your beliefs, sustain your motivation during challenging times, and shape how you interact with others in the movement. They remind you why you're fighting and how you plan to enact change.

For those drawn to activism, a common core value might be justice, equity, or community. Such values don't just influence the kind of work you choose to do; they compel you to get involved, not sit on the sidelines, but actively participate in the struggle for change.

By defining and understanding your core values, you prepare yourself to be not just an activist but a centered, grounded, and effective one. Your values will not only choose your battles for you but also arm you with the persistence needed to continue the fight. This self-awareness ensures that your activism is not just an external endeavor but a profound expression of your deepest self, making your efforts even more powerful and your resolve unshakeable.

Engaging in 'good trouble' isn't just a choice but a necessity for real change. This term, inspired by the legendary John Lewis, encapsulates what it means to be an activist committed to justice. It's about stirring the pot, not for the sake of trouble, but to challenge the status quo and catalyze progress.

Early in my career, I encountered a glaring injustice where the women at my workplace were underpaid and undervalued. After witnessing this disparity for some time, I organized a meeting for the women to voice their concerns and discuss strategies for better treatment. Despite the purity of our intentions, not everyone was supportive.

One colleague informed our boss about the meeting, leading to a confrontation where I was labeled an agitator. I remember the sting of those words, feeling diminished and misunderstood. I wasn't trying to create problems; I was trying to solve them.

Later, sharing this experience with a close friend helped me see the situation differently. She reminded me that agitation is at the heart of activism. It's about highlighting injustices and striving for solutions. Her words helped reshape my understanding of my actions: I was not just causing trouble; I was creating 'good trouble,' engaging in necessary activism to foster change.

Speaking your truth, especially as an activist, often has various consequences. These can range from personal attacks and social exclusion to being sidelined in important discussions or decisions. In the current climate of movements like MeToo and Black Lives Matter, while activism might appear trendy, the reality of living out these principles is anything but simple.

I have faced everything from name-calling and loss of support to being ostracized. Often, ideas I proposed were adopted without acknowledgment, or I was not invited to the decision-making table. These experiences, though disheartening, have underscored the importance of resilience and commitment to one's principles in the face of adversity.

Even as an activist, the pressure to conform can be intense. Whether it's pressure from non-activist friends who wish you would *"let it rest for once"* or activist peers who may think you're not doing enough, standing firm in your beliefs is a continuous challenge. It's crucial to remain true to your core values, even when it means standing alone.

Developing a thick skin is part of the journey. Accepting that not everyone will agree with or support your cause is essential. It's about understanding that being an activist means sometimes being out of step with not just adversaries, but friends, family, and colleagues.

As a centered activist, your voice is your most powerful tool. Knowing and speaking your truth from a centered place—a position not of arrogance or vindictiveness but of commitment to truth—is crucial. This stance is not about elevating oneself but lifting the issues and advocating for change.

According to an article from GotQuestions.org, the definition of objective truth is that it corresponds with reality and is true for everyone, regardless of whether they agree with it. Historically, this was simply known as "truth." However, in today's climate of disinformation, where phenomena like Q-ANON or false narratives such as those propagated by Trump about voter fraud can incite significant events like the Capitol uprising, "truth" has morphed into something that often just means agreement with one's own views.

As Vladimir Lenin famously said in this context, *"A lie told often enough becomes the truth."*

This manipulation of truth doesn't just impact political spheres; it seeps into every facet of society, significantly influencing young minds still forming their perceptions of the world.

In my own journey as an activist, the relationship between truth and justice has always been fraught with challenges.

In today's world, where tribal thinking and strict party lines dominate, identifying the true essence of facts becomes daunting. Here, it's important to distinguish between mere facts and a more profound truth that resonates with our core values. The challenge lies in recognizing that while facts are concrete, our perceptions and biases often influence the truth.

Truth, even truth that is objectively linked to reality, holds immense power, and unfortunately, there are entities intent on distorting it for their own benefit. These distortions are systematically woven into our societal fabric, perpetuating harmful ideologies such as white supremacy. Living under this constant barrage of falsehoods, many have inadvertently internalized these lies and double-speak, sometimes creating a "counter-truth" as a psychological defense mechanism despite its detachment from actual facts.

Speaking your truth in such a hostile environment means consciously stepping away from the chaos of popular culture and its misinformation. It involves ensuring that your information sources extend beyond the echo chambers of social media. Engaging in meaningful conversations with real people who are actively involved in tangible work on the ground is vital. It also necessitates a rigorous practice of analyzing and critiquing information, irrespective of the source.

To commit to 'good trouble-' or be a centered activist in this landscape, one must navigate these treacherous waters with resilience and a deep commitment to integrity. Speaking your truth isn't merely about voicing your opinions; it's about steadfastly adhering to values that uphold justice and equity, even when faced with opposition or isolation. This commitment to truth ultimately fosters real change and drives the social justice movements forward.

One of the most crucial and ongoing aspects of activism involves continuous self-reflection and honesty. This means recognizing that just like anyone else, we are not immune to harboring prejudiced, racist, sexist, elitist, homophobic, revisionist, or tribal attitudes. If we fail to examine our own behaviors and beliefs continually, there's a real risk that we could become the very type of person we're fighting against. This, dear reader, is a fundamental truth.

So, how do we ensure we align with our values and not perpetuate the problems we aim to solve?

It starts with actively and personally engaging in the communities affected by the issues we champion. For example, I once participated in a grassroots movement at a big box store, where workers advocated for better wages and conditions. Being on the ground, hearing their stories firsthand, and sharing their daily experiences reinforced my commitment to the cause and helped keep my perspectives grounded in the reality of the people I wanted to support.

We must also continuously check our own shortcomings and strive for improvement. This not only enhances our credibility but also strengthens the impact of our activism. Engaging with real people in real situations tests our beliefs and methods and deepens our understanding and empathy—a critical component of effective advocacy.

Step 4: Speaking Your Truth in a Complicated World

Speaking your truth isn't always straightforward, especially in the complex terrain of activism, where multiple voices and agendas often collide. It requires discernment to know when to speak, what to say, and how to say it. It also involves listening deeply to others, as genuine dialogue can enhance understanding and refine your perspectives.

Moreover, speaking your truth responsibly involves acknowledging the impact of your words and actions on others. It's about striving for honesty without causing harm and assertiveness without aggression. This balance is crucial in activism, where words can be powerful tools for change or unintended weapons of division.

George Orwell famously said, *"Freedom is the right to tell people what they do not want to hear."*

This belief underscores the importance of truth in our work. We must learn to comfortably and confidently speak truth to power, prepared for the repercussions that often follow.

As activists, we must embody the change we wish to see by living out our truths and continuously checking our alignment with our core values. This ongoing process, while hard, keeps us true to ourselves and our missions and inspires those we serve and represent. Speaking truth to power involves making tough decisions that may not always be popular but are necessary for the greater good. Embracing this role of igniting 'good trouble' is essential for driving lasting change.

Speaking truth to power is a formidable challenge; it isolates you and often provokes fierce opposition. Sometimes, this means confronting external adversaries as well as those within your own ranks, which can be even more daunting.

In my experience, activists and organizers—who often pride themselves on being "woke"—sometimes fall into the trap of believing they have a monopoly on justice and the correct methods of achieving it. We see this manifested in not only being quick to criticize external forces that oppose our ideals but we have even more intense scrutiny and antagonism within our own organizations and affinity groups. It's common to witness harsher, more destructive criticism directed at fellow activists diverging from the group's consensus. This internal conflict can be more vicious and personally damaging than disputes with external entities.

Why does this happen?

Over the years, I've pondered this question extensively. It might stem from internalized oppression—the notion that we do not fully accept or love ourselves, leading us to project these insecurities onto others in our group. Alternatively, it could be a deep-seated distrust developed from past betrayals by those who seemed to share our values but ultimately disappointed or deceived us. This skepticism can make us wary of even our closest allies.

Another possibility is the inherent nature of being an organizer or activist. Choosing to be a truth-teller and agitator is not a role that switches off once the protest ends or the meeting ends. It is embedded in our identity; it's part of our very essence.

Consequently, we apply the same fervor and critical approach to our personal interactions as we do in our public engagements. This relentless advocacy can strain relationships and often lead to fallout if the intensity of our convictions does not easily coexist with compromise or differing opinions.

In such a high-stakes environment, the concept of grace becomes essential. We cannot be perpetually on the attack and expect to thrive. This constant state of conflict is unsustainable and can lead to burnout, disillusionment, or worse.

We must balance standing firm in our beliefs and allowing space for dissent and dialogue within our ranks. This balance does not mean diluting our principles but rather fostering an environment where diverse opinions can coexist and enrich the movement.

Grace in activism means acknowledging that we are all working towards a common goal, albeit sometimes with different perspectives on how to get there. It involves giving each other the benefit of the doubt and handling internal conflicts with the same compassion and understanding we ask of the broader world. Without this grace, we risk alienating valuable allies and weakening our collective efforts.

Moreover, we must consider what part of ourselves we lose when we engage in constant conflict, whether as the aggressor or the recipient. Each skirmish leaves a mark; each battle scars us in some way. If we are not careful, we risk losing sight of why we became activists in the first place—to create a just, compassionate, and equitable society.

In conclusion, speaking truth to power, externally or within our internal working groups, requires courage, resilience, and, importantly, grace. These qualities ensure that our activism remains effective and true to its purpose, preventing us from becoming the forces we aim to change. This delicate balance is not easily achieved, but it is essential for the sustainability of both our movements and ourselves.

Chapter 10: Developing a Spiritual Practice

Raised with a strong Christian foundation, I've always been drawn to teachings emphasizing service, compassion, and justice. These principles have significantly shaped my approach to activism, instilling a sense of duty to advocate for those marginalized by society.

My faith has made me want my vocation and advocation to be congruent. I am happy that I have been able to live out my faith in tangible ways throughout my professional career.

In this chapter, I talk about religion and spirituality, so I want to define each. Religion is a structured system of beliefs and practices often shared by a community or group. Spirituality is a personal practice that involves a search for meaning in life and a connection to something greater than oneself. It can include focusing on the present moment, the soul, and connection with others and nature. Spirituality is a universal human experience.

While spirituality is a part of religion, one can be spiritual without being religious. I am both religious and spiritual, and some of my spiritual practices are also tenets of my religious faith.

Richard Foster is the author of the book, *"Celebration of Discipline: The Paths to Spiritual Growth."* In its opening pages, he wrote that:

"Superficiality is the curse of our age. The doctrine of instant satisfaction is a primary spiritual problem. The desperate need today is not a greater number of intelligent people or gifted people but for deep people."

Foster posits that a spiritual life calls us to move beyond surface living and urges us to be the answer to a hollow world. Foster uses the term spiritual discipline rather than spiritual practice. Both terms refer to activities or actions done regularly that lead to spiritual development and growth. He organizes the book based on inward, outward, and corporate disciplines. I read his book in 1988, a year after I created my nonprofit and ten years after it was first published. I remember learning about many of the disciplines he discussed in childhood but not practicing them. His book helped to change that.

Like my Christian faith, spirituality has also profoundly influenced and sustained my activism. It serves not just as solace but as a fundamental framework for my beliefs and actions, especially as I navigate the complexities of social change. In this chapter, I share some of the spiritual practices that are powerful tools in my arsenal to keep my mind tough and my heart tender.

Social justice work is hard and very demanding; it is easy to get lost in it and lose yourself.

I advocate that activists engage in spiritual practices, whether religiously based or not, that help them stay balanced, find joy, and heal.

Maintaining a spiritual practice while engaging in activism cannot be overstated. It offers a reservoir of strength and perspective, especially when confronted with the immense challenges of changing entrenched systems of injustice. Spirituality provides a framework for understanding the interconnectedness of all life and compels me to act with integrity and compassion.

In narrating my story, I uncover the intricate ways in which spirituality supports and propels my activism efforts. This spiritual foundation enriches my understanding of the world, enhances my engagements, and deepens my commitment to creating a more just and compassionate society. Through this exploration, I aim to demonstrate how deeply intertwined our spiritual lives are with our actions in the world, reinforcing the belief that personal transformation and societal change are mutually reinforcing endeavors.

From the very beginning, spirituality has offered me a lens through which I view the world. It's not just about personal solace or retreat from the stresses of activism; it's about empowering myself to engage deeply with issues that matter. My spiritual beliefs energize me, infuse my actions with purpose, and remind me that my work is part of a larger narrative of human struggle and resilience.

Moreover, my Christian upbringing instilled a strong sense of justice and the belief that service to others is a sacred duty. These teachings have been a guiding light in my activism, inspiring me to advocate tirelessly for those who are marginalized and oppressed.

I engage in spiritual practices as a commitment to personal growth and introspection. I spend a lot of time in quiet reflection, which helps me stay grounded amidst the chaos that often comes with social activism.

My primary spiritual practice is conversations with God, better known as prayers. I have an intimate relationship with God, so I talk to God, pouring out my heart and sharing unashamedly. Prayer has always been a refuge for me—a way to step back, reflect, and seek guidance when the obstacles seem insurmountable. Whether it was struggling with the direction of my advocacy work or facing personal trials, prayer offered me clarity and peace amidst the turmoil. It's like conversing with a trusted advisor who always steers you toward your true north.

Journaling, meditative practices, and simple, quiet moments are not just breaks from my work—they are essential to my spirituality, replenishing my spirit and preparing me to face new challenges.

But my spiritual journey hasn't been confined to the practices I grew up with, which are listed above. Curiosity about how others find peace and purpose led me to explore various spiritual practices.

One key practice I've embraced is mindfulness, which allows me to maintain presence and awareness amidst the chaos of everyday life. This tool helps me stay grounded, ensuring my actions align with my values and remain connected to the human experience. Mindfulness teaches me to observe without judgment, to respond rather than react, and to try to handle each situation with thoughtfulness and care.

My exploration of mindfulness and other spiritual practices has not replaced but rather enriched my Christian faith. I have incorporate elements of these practices into my life, enhancing my resilience and broadening my approach to activism. This synthesis of spiritual insights has fortified my commitment to social justice, equipping me with tools that help maintain my well-being while vigorously pursuing the cause of equity and justice.

Diving deeper into how spirituality shapes my activism, it's clear that my connection to God and my Christian faith profoundly influence how I view and interact with the world. Describing my spirituality in broad terms, it's a guiding force that permeates every aspect of my existence, steering me through life's many challenges and victories. Yet, in a more specific sense, it translates into daily practices and beliefs rooted in Christianity, where I see God not as an entity of retribution but as a Liberator—a source of freedom and justice.

I'm not rigid in my practices. I pray, read the Bible, and attend church, yet I hold onto the flexibility that life sometimes demands. Suppose travel or life's unpredictability keeps me from church. In that case, I find peace in knowing that my prayer—my conversations with God—remains intact, unfettered by the confines of physical spaces or strict schedules.

As an activist, I never feel like there is enough time. I am often running like a hamster on a wheel. It is exhausting and for a long time, I was always exhausted. One of the practices that I have undertaken is to slow down and see and experience time differently. Not just on a practical level where I acknowledge that I cannot work nonstop or refuse to go on vacation. But in terms of the evolution of my understanding of time—from the rigid, sequential order of Chronos to the profound, opportune moments of Kairos which has been nothing short of transformative. This shift has deepened my spiritual practice and honed my intuition, allowing me to embrace the fluidity of life with both arms wide open.

Chronos is a term used to refer to a specific amount of time, such as a day or an hour. Chronos is that relentless tick-tock, a schedule-packed existence many of us subscribe to. It's the deadlines, the meetings, and the ever-present hustle. Author Tricia Hershey speaks of Chronos' time when she talks about "grind culture" in her book *Rest is Resistance: A Manifesto.*

Living in Chronos, I constantly chased after time, trying to capture it in my hands only to watch it slip through like sand. It was a relentless cycle that often left me more exhausted than fulfilled.

Then came my introduction to Kairos, which means right time, season, or opportunity in Greek. In my faith tradition, Kairos means the appointed time for the purpose of God, the time when God acts. Kairos is—those perfect moments when time seems to stand still, offering opportunities for significant, though often unexpected, insights and transformations. Kairos is about quality, not quantity. It's about making the most of the present and embracing opportunities at just the right time. Learning to recognize and appreciate these moments has enriched my personal life and invigorated my activism with a renewed sense of purpose and passion.

This transition has also led me to prioritize deeper spiritual practices. I've embraced meditation and contemplative prayer, which goes beyond just giving God a laundry list of things God needs to handle for me. These practices help me sift through daily noise and focus on what truly matters. Often giving me the strength to continue my work and the grace to navigate the complexities of life.

Speaking of grace, its impact on both my personal and professional life has been immeasurable. Grace is not something you earn; it is unearned and freely given. Some practical ways grace manifests in my life are gratitude, self-compassion, apologizing, letting things go, getting rid of my perfection practice, which is hard, and just letting myself and people be human.

Grace is this beautiful, unearned favor that manifests in small gestures and monumental acts. It's found in the supportive words of a friend when I'm feeling down, the unexpected resolution of a complex issue at work, or the serene stillness of early morning hours before the world awakes. These instances of grace remind me of the beauty and interconnectedness of life.

Moreover, grace brings moments of renewal and restoration when least expected but most needed. There have been countless times when I've felt depleted, ready to give up, and right then, a moment of grace emerges—a chance encounter, a piece of good news, a breakthrough in my work. These moments recharge my spirit and reaffirm my purpose, reminding me that I am not alone in this journey.

Recognizing these unexpected moments of grace has taught me to be more open and receptive to the unexpected. It has shown me that renewal and restoration are not always planned or predictable but often come just at the right time, offering new perspectives and fresh energy.

Another crucial aspect of my spiritual toolbox is regular engagement with nature. Nature is not just a place to escape to but a powerful teacher of resilience and renewal. Whether walking through a forest, listening to a stream, leaning against a tree, or simply sitting in a park, nature's rhythms help me connect with the life cycle, reminding me of the world's natural order and my place within it. These moments in nature are not just refreshing escapes but pivotal experiences that recalibrate my understanding of time and priority, teaching me lessons of patience, growth, and the impermanence of life's trials.

Self-mastery, a continual goal in my spiritual and personal development, involves what the culture calls check yourself before you wreck yourself. This disciplined practice includes not engaging in negative public or private self-talk,learning how to control my behavior, and demonstrating that I am strong enough to be gentle. These practices strengthen my willpower and enhance my capacity to control my thoughts and emotions, which is crucial in both personal development and effective activism. Through self-mastery, I am learning to harness my inner strength to face external challenges, ensuring I act from a place of love, integrity, and purpose.

I believe love is the most powerful force in the universe, and using love as a driving force in my life and activism takes work. Love is a spiritual principle and practice that demands that I recognize my own worth, the worth of others, and our interconnectedness.

I use yoga as a platform for my physical, mental, and emotional wellness. I have a primarily home-based yoga practice. COVID shut down yoga studios, and although yoga studios are open now, I have never gotten back to doing yoga in community settings unless it is outside. What I think I enjoy almost as much as the stretching, breath work, and centering of yoga is when, at the end of class, the instructor closes the practice by saying Namaste, which means I see, I recognize the divine in you. All that to say, how can we do this work of self and world transformation if there is no agape love, wanting the best, and extending help or goodwill toward another as a part of the work?

As I have grown deeper in my spiritual journey, the balance between active engagement and reflective withdrawal has become a central theme. Spiritual practice is not just a refuge from the storm of life; it is an active engagement with the inner self that complements and informs my activism. It's about integrating spiritual wisdom with intellectual pursuits to achieve holistic well-being.

This integration is vital for any activist. It's too easy to be consumed by our causes' urgency or become overwhelmed by the injustices we fight against. Spiritual practices counterbalance this, providing spaces for recharge and reflection, which is essential for long-term sustainability in activism.

Moreover, these practices help cultivate a broader perspective, allowing me to see beyond the immediate to the interconnectedness of all actions and their deeper impacts. They foster a sense of peace and acceptance, equipping me with the emotional and psychological strength to continue the work, even when progress seems slow or invisible.

As we move forward in this narrative, the importance of spiritual practice for maintaining balance and resilience in activism becomes increasingly clear. It's about weaving together the threads of spiritual insights and day-to-day experiences to create a stronger, more resilient fabric of activism.

In essence, the call to integrate spiritual wisdom with intellectual pursuits is to enrich our lives with depth and meaning. It's a journey towards holistic well-being that enhances personal growth and amplifies our effectiveness as agents of change in the world. This integration ensures that we are well-informed and passionate about our causes and wise, compassionate, and balanced in our approach, making us better leaders and humans.

Chapter 11: Accepting Setbacks and Refusing Defeat

"The river may be wide, but it can be crossed."

-Ivorian proverb

"You can fall, but you can rise also."

-Angelique Kidjo

I own a small house in an urban neighborhood in Atlanta. When I first purchased it, everything was new and pristine. However, over the last 25+ years, it has needed various repairs. Things have broken, worn out, or become misaligned. The roof needed replacing, window casings had to be fixed, and plumbing issues arose. Specific projects included installing a new HVAC system, replacing outdated electrical wiring, fixing a leaking basement, and repairing a sagging deck.

Despite these challenges, I don't see the repair work as a failure but rather as the expected maintenance required over time for a structure that has stood the test of two decades. I want it to last many more decades, so I have to spend time and resources shoring it up, providing the support it needs to remain intact and viable, usable as a place for me and others to gather, to work, and most importantly, live.

Repairing the house was a financial setback, especially when some projects were large, unplanned, and not fully covered by insurance. However, this is also a reality of homeownership. Though costly, each repair ensures the home's longevity and safety.

Is repairing the house a setback?

It depends on how you look at it.

From one perspective, the continuous need for repairs can feel like a setback, draining financial resources and sometimes causing stress. However, from another perspective, these repairs are investments in the future. They ensure that the house remains a safe and comfortable place to live.

Whenever I fix something, I'm reminded of the importance of resilience and maintenance for homes and life. Just as my house requires periodic attention and care, so do our personal and professional lives. We all encounter financial, emotional, or physical setbacks that require us to adjust, repair, and move forward.

For instance, when the roof needed replacing, I remember the stress of finding a reliable contractor, the noise and mess during the replacement and dealing with the insurance company to ensure that as much of the cost was covered as possible. Yet, when the work was completed, the house was better protected from the elements, and I knew I had made a wise investment in its future.

These experiences taught me valuable lessons about preparedness and flexibility. Homeownership, much like life, is full of unforeseen challenges. We can plan and save, but sometimes life throws curveballs, and we must handle them as they come. Each repair, while a setback in the short term, contributes to the long-term stability and comfort of the home.

So often, people mistake setbacks for defeats. I've faced many setbacks in my life; had I allowed them, they would have been the source of my defeat. For example, when I began my legal career, I failed the Georgia bar exam.

Not passing the bar was devastating for me. I had never experienced such a public failure before. I call it public because all my friends had passed. Folks in my office knew, and it required me to get other lawyers to sign off on my work. My family knew, too.

I had to dig deep on that one. I felt like giving up, but I couldn't. After the last failure in Georgia, I accepted my setback and decided there had to be another way. And there was. I needed to start fresh and take the bar in a new place, so I began to look at other southern states.

I had a friend in Mississippi, so I applied to take their bar exam. The night before the exam, I was alone in my cheap hotel room and started freaking out: crying, screaming, begging God just to let me pass because, if I didn't, I felt like I could never move on in my life. That wasn't true.

But thank God, I passed.

You couldn't have told me then that I would only practice law for a short time—only three and a half to four years— and that the title I used to tell the world who I was professionally would not be an attorney. What I didn't realize then (and I guess we often don't see things clearly as we go through them) is that the GA bar failure, the loss of friends who didn't see me on their level anymore, the humiliation in front of my colleagues, and the comments by other lawyers, including the ones who hadn't passed the first time themselves, were all part of a setback that prepared me to stay on a very difficult course for almost 40 years.

Through that experience, I developed an inner strength I have had to call on repeatedly. It has been my constant companion, especially in the early years when people weren't concerned about prisoners; not that they truly are now, but they were really in a *"lock them up and throw away the key"* mentality back then.

Society's lack of concern for prisoners extended to their children, who were practically invisible, and due to our sexist society, women in prison got the least amount of attention. I remember my founding board president, Dr. Paula Dressel, and I went to Washington during the Reagan administration to meet with Otis Bowen, the head of Health and Human Services. We never met him, but the person who did meet with us instead told us women were "out of fashion."

That attitude was prevalent, as was the notion that women who had gone to prison were unfit mothers just because they had been incarcerated.

In my professional journey, setbacks were numerous. For instance, our organization faced financial hardships that led to program cuts and staff layoffs. Despite these challenges, we are still standing today.

One of the most significant setbacks involved our socially responsible fundraising policy, which I championed because I wanted to do socially responsible work. I wanted the work to benefit the individuals we served and society at large.

I created, and the board approved, a fundraising policy that did not allow us to take money from companies' or foundations whose primary products were connected to the pathways to prison for many of the people we served. In reality, that meant not taking money from the alcohol industry, the subsidiaries of the adult entertainment market, or the lottery. Sometimes, I wondered if this was the right decision, especially during financial crises.

But in retrospect, it was the best decision I made. It protected our agency's core values and maintained the integrity of our mission.

When times were hard, I even chose not to take a salary so that the funds could be used to support others in the organization. Though financially challenging, this decision aligned with my commitment to the mission and ensured our work could continue. Over time, I found ways to support myself through consulting, allowing me to maintain my dedication to the cause while securing my financial stability.

Our organization, initially named *Aid to Imprisoned Mothers* (AIM), faced additional challenges due to its name. While adding "Children" to the name helped raise funds, it also increased the stigma, leading us to rebrand as Foreverfamily in 2007. This name change reflected our mission of supporting children with incarcerated mothers and fathers and emphasized the enduring bonds of family.

Despite these setbacks, our organization has supported approximately 45,000 children. This support has taken many forms, from providing transportation for prison visits and offering summer camps to running after-school programs and assisting with educational and career development. We've also helped families in practical ways, such as writing letters to social service agencies, referring families to other community-based programs that could meet needs Foreverfamily was not designed to address, providing back-to-school supplies, and offering scholarships.

The success of our organization can be seen in the lives we've touched. The children we supported became teachers, nonprofit founders, military personnel, retail workers, and more. Pre-COVID, only 6% of the kids we worked with ended up in juvenile or adult facilities, a statistic I am incredibly proud of. Our team's hard work, dedication, and the supportive community that rallied around us made this success possible.

Being a Black woman and starting a nonprofit that addressed a "hidden in plain sight" issue at the age of 28, I faced numerous obstacles. My age, race, and gender were all factors that could have easily defeated me. However, I refused to be defeated. This refusal was rooted in the experiences I shared with you earlier and deeply ingrained in the values I learned as a child. We were taught to understand and appreciate the struggles and triumphs of our ancestors. When faced with challenges, I would often reflect on the immense hardships they overcame and draw strength from their resilience. If they could endure such monumental struggles, surely I could handle my setbacks and keep moving forward.

Resilience is the thread that runs through all my experiences with defeat. Every setback that knocked me down only made me stronger and more prepared for the next challenge. The setbacks varied, requiring different skills and strategies to overcome, but the perseverance remained constant.

The hardest setbacks always involved people. Losing a grant, for instance, meant losing a valuable team member who did excellent work. This was not just a professional setback but a personal one, as it meant the rest of us had to take on even more responsibilities. These losses were deeply felt, but they never defeated us. We adapted, we persevered, and we continued to push forward.

Some setbacks were beyond my control, such as the personal tragedies of the families we served. Mothers getting cancer in prison, fathers dying while incarcerated—these were heartbreaking realities that I couldn't change. While these were significant setbacks for the families, my goal was always to walk beside them, not in front or behind, and to support them through their struggles. I believed deeply in a better day coming, which fueled my work and kept me moving forward.

I see even the grimmest situations with hope. This belief in a better tomorrow drives my work and my approach to setbacks. Accepting setbacks doesn't mean accepting defeat. It means learning from each experience, growing stronger, and continuing the fight for a better future. This resilience keeps me going, and I hope to instill it in others.

Epilogue

Throughout the writing of this book, I have traveled down memory lane, sharing things I remember vividly, as well as some I had forgotten or wanted to. All of them are a part of my journey. I believe that good and right will triumph in the end. My faith tradition teaches that my mind thinks it, and my heart feels it. If we unite and each of us does our part, we can change things.

We have to work as if our lives, and others, depend on it.

They do!

I want to share a final story that illustrates my point.

I remember the shooting and bombing at Columbine High School in 1999. As a country and as a world community, we were all devastated. Months later, I was in Colorado with a colleague on a consulting project in Longmont. After our work ended, we drove an hour and 10 minutes to Littleton, where the high school is located. We went to the school grounds to stand in solidarity with that community by physically showing up to bear witness not to the deaths but to life and love.

As we stood there, we were like so many people who were on the grounds, overcome with grief and sadness. Neither of us had ever been to the school before nor knew anyone who lived in Littleton or had children at Columbine High School, but that didn't matter. We understand the human condition of death and the pain, sorrow, and grief that follows.

We just stood there, not talking to each other or to anyone else. We prayed and wept silently, believing for something different, more affirming for children, families, and the many lives destroyed on April 20. Yes, our presence was a protest, and it was also two human beings expressing love as a balm for that community and our world. Our humanity was on full display, and we left Columbine different from when we came.

Did the mass shootings stop?

No, they continue to this day, and their frequency has increased so much that some of us are immune to them. They are just another everyday occurrence.

My colleague and I weren't there because we thought what we did that day on the hill overlooking the aftermath of a mass shooting would instantly change everything. We were there because we knew that, as members of the human family, we had to show up and do something. We engaged in small-scale activism. Yet that small act of protest has deepened my commitment to supporting folks working to end gun violence and prevents me from thinking when I hear about an active shooter, *'Oh, it's just another shooting; they happen all the time.'*

I cannot act like business as usual when I hear of a mass shooting.

I have worked on the same issue for almost 40 years.

Are children still the collateral damage of our criminal legal system?

Yes.

But 45,000 know they are important because some of us decided to do something. Thousands of people who worked, interned, served on the agency's board, and volunteered made a difference and created social change. That is powerful, and it is what movement-building looks like.

Many people in the categories above only stayed at Foreverfamily for a short term or just a part of their careers. Other than me, the longest-running staff person stayed for nine years. I had not expected people to come and stay with us on a full-time basis for decades. My hope was what happened. People would come, contribute, and learn about what it looks like to make change and what it feels like to be the change.

I say be the change because more than we realize, the work of justice isn't just about everybody else. It is about us – each of us – dealing with who we are and the privileges we hold - whether it is whiteness, maleness, education, income, citizenship, being the first, having a long history or experience with an issue or a host of other privileges that can get in the way of the work and separate us from not unite us with others.

The Black woman educator Marva Collins said we enter to learn and exit to serve. I agree, and the plan was always that people would move on in their lives, work on other issues, and while doing so, always carry what they learned at Foreverfamily about how to take up the work of social change through a lens that focused on removing barriers that diminish and disregard people's right to self-determination and respect.

People who had served with us would endeavor, whether on a short-term project, a long-term campaign, or at the moment, to co-labor with others from a place that was anti-racist, sexist, and elitist. They would challenge others around them to be equity-seeking and people-loving. Most importantly, they would, when the going got tough, remember never to give up.

I am deeply encouraged by the many women, men, and young people involved at Foreverfamily on various levels who are disbursed locally, regionally, nationally, and across international waters who engage in good trouble. I am grateful that my consulting business allows me to partner with a diverse team of people who share my commitment to making change. Together, we work with some of the most gifted and talented activists on the Deep South's frontlines, tackling tough issues and getting results.

I will always believe we can create a world where we can live out our highest ideals. I am committed to fighting for that until my last breath.

Bernice Johnson Reagon, who was a founding member of the Freedom Singers[12], organized by the Student Non-

---

[12] Wikipedia contributors. (2024, August 16). The Freedom Singers. Wikipedia. https://en.wikipedia.org/wiki/The_Freedom_Singers

violent Coordinating Committee (SNCC)[13] in the Albany Movement[14] for civil rights[15] in Georgia, and also the founder of the a cappella group *Sweet Honey and the Rock*, expresses my sentiments in the lyrics she wrote for Ella's Song which she later pinned to music.

Ella's Song

We who believe in freedom cannot rest

We who believe in freedom cannot rest until it comes

Until the killing of black men, black mothers' sons

Is as important as the killing of white men, white mothers' sons

That which touches me most is that I had a chance to work with people

Passing on to others that which was passed on to me

To me, young people come first, they have the courage where we fail

And if I can but shed some light as they carry us through the gale

The older I get, the better I know that the secret of my going on

---

[13] Wikipedia contributors. (2024b, September 4). Student Nonviolent Coordinating Committee. Wikipedia. https://en.wikipedia.org/wiki/Student_Non-violent_Coordinating_Committee

[14] Wikipedia contributors. (2024a, June 1). Albany Movement. Wikipedia. https://en.wikipedia.org/wiki/Albany_Movement

[15] Wikipedia contributors. (2024c, August 28). *Civil rights movement*. Wikipedia. https://en.wikipedia.org/wiki/Civil_Rights_Movement

Is when the reins are in the hands of the young, who dare to run against the storm

Not needing to clutch for power, not needing the light just to shine on me

I need to be one in the number as we stand against tyranny

Struggling myself don't mean a whole lot, I've come to realize

That teaching others to stand up and fight is the only way my struggle survives

I'm a woman who speaks in a voice, and I must be heard
At times, I can be quite difficult. I'll bow to no man's word

We who believe in freedom cannot rest

We who believe in freedom cannot rest until it comes.

Bernice Reagon, who died on July 16, 2024, wrote that song during the Civil Rights Movement to honor another of my sheroes, Ella Baker. Ella's Song[16] is an anthem, a meditation on the ultimate lesson of the freedom fight passed down generationally that is meant to be spoken boldly out loud or under one's breath as the situation demands to empower both our purpose and our resolve.

Our challenge is to live in this world with our humanity on full display, which means we each, in some way, large or small, must ensure that we leave this world better than we found it.

To do that, we need a tough mind and a tender heart.

---

[16] ELLA'S SONG / ALL by MW -. (n.d.). Golden Bridge Community Choir. https://goldenbridgechoir.com/track/2377080/ella-s-song-all

www.ingramcontent.com/pod-product-compliance
Lightning Source LLC
Chambersburg PA
CBHW061259120726
48001CB00001B/375